HIGHWAYMEN

All eyes were turned to see Blueskin wrestling furiously with Wild, the Thief-taker
(*See page 206*)

HIGHWAYMEN

a book of gallant rogues
by Charles J. Finger
with illustrations from
woodblocks
by Paul Honoré

Essay Index Reprint Series

BOOKS FOR LIBRARIES PRESS
FREEPORT, NEW YORK

To
A. T. SIEGEL
OF
ST. LOUIS, MO.,
AND
R. B. CUNNINGHAME GRAHAM
OF SCOTLAND,
GALLANT GENTLEMEN, BOTH.

CONTENTS

	PAGE
COLONEL THOMAS BLOOD	1
BLOOD'S WAGER	3
BLOOD'S GREAT THEFT	18
JACK SHEPPARD	41
DICK TURPIN	77
CLAUDE DUVAL	117
A NET OF LOOSE FISH	173
JAMES MACLEAN	178
JONATHAN WILD	197
BILL OF TIERRA DEL FUEGO	211

THE ILLUSTRATIONS

All eyes were turned to see Blueskin wrestling furiously with Wild, the Thief-taker . . . . . *Frontispiece*

                                                          FACING PAGE

Ormond lay on the scaffold floor, his arms bound, and the hangman's rope about his neck 16

Jack Sheppard on the road to Tyburn 48

A touch of the spur and Black Bess rose to it . . . 106

"So I have found Midas and persuaded him" . . . 140

"Into the river with your swords," he commanded . . 186

From end to end of the boat he went, striking, cursing, threatening 218

In the saddle was the wounded and tortured Gonzales . 246

COLONEL THOMAS BLOOD

BLOOD'S WAGER

IT was a dark December night except for the faint glimmer of a few stars in a cloudy sky, when the coach of my lord the Duke of Ormond, Lord Lieutenant of Ireland, was stopped by a lone highwayman at Edgeware. Perhaps the pate of the armed guard who sat on the box beside the coachman was heavy with drink, and perhaps he was asleep, but certain it is that neither he nor the mounted man who followed the coach was prepared to offer resistance. Out from beneath the poplars that lined the road cantered the horseman, masked and cloaked, and, as he drew his sword, he cried, loud enough for the man inside the coach to hear:

"Let no man stir, or speak, on peril of his life!"

He spurred his horse, then, to the side of the coach horses, and, with a single slash of his blade, cut the traces on one side and bade the coachman throw the reins across the backs of his steeds, which he did without any ado. Seeing how matters stood, the mounted rear guard turned bridle and fled. As the highwayman rode to the coach door, the guard on the box seat made some stir and produced from the folds of his cloak a heavy pistol.

"Man, are you mad?" asked the highwayman. "What peril are you minded to run to protect such a fellow as your master within?" At that, the fellow threw his pistol into the roadway and made no further move, but sat through what followed with folded arms.

By then, the passenger in the coach was well awake, and, taking in the situation, made himself busy. Before the highwayman had said a word, he thrust his hand through the open coach window, holding out a well-filled purse.

"Your jewels, too," demanded the highwayman, and, with a sigh that was almost a groan, all that was of value, his rings, his diamond hat clasp and his gold chain, was handed over.

"There is more," said the knight of the road. "The rest that you have, I want."

"But I have no more," declared the man in the coach. "My money and my jewels you have. What more is there?"

"Your papers. The paper with the list of names of those you have condemned to die in Ireland. Give me the papers, for I am not minded that men should die at your word. Besides, they are honest men, who have been despoiled. So haste."

"But the papers are the King's," protested the man in the coach.

"It is far better that the King should lose papers than good men, and I have sworn that those men shall not die," said the horseman in a crisp voice, laying his sword-point on the window's edge.

My lord was evidently not cowed, although outmastered. In an icy voice he said: "Well and good. But this to you, my fine fellow. May you not long escape the rope on which you seem to have set your heart." So saying, he handed to the highwayman a bundle of papers.

"And now, *bonne fortune,*" said the robber with a laugh, as he thrust the booty away beneath his cloak. "As for the rope, I'll wager that it is about your throat before it is about mine, my lord."

There was a short silence, then the man in the coach murmured, "Things would go ill indeed, in this land, when a titled name stood at a gallows tree."

"And yet, I'll wager, my lord, all these jewels against the lives of the men whose names you have listed for hanging in Ireland, that before twenty-four hours you will stand at Tyburn—"

"To see you hanged," interrupted the Duke of Ormond.

"Not so. But with a rope collar about your neck," laughed the other.

Emotion deep and angry stirred in the robbed man. He thrust his face out of the coach window though in doing so he put his breast within an inch of the sword's point.

"Away with you for an ill-bred varlet!" he cried. "I have had enough of the rough side of your tongue." Then he cursed his coachman and his guard for cowardly fellows and bade them see about getting on their way.

"Soon, then, shall we meet again," said the highwayman, turning in his saddle. So, laughing heartily, he shook his rein and started off. But he reined in after a little and said, "For your promptitude, my lord Duke, my thanks, for my business is of a kind that will not endure waiting." Then he was off, with a merry clatter of hoofs, on the way to London.

—2—

On the night following, sedan chair after sedan chair deposited people in front of the fashionable house of Mrs. Bennett, and the ragged crowd about the door was somewhat impatiently waiting, expecting something. My lord this, and my lady that were recognized and cheered, or hissed, according to their popularity or the reverse, as they walked from chair to house door. Of all who passed along the little lane of sightseers, the Duke of Buckingham in gold-laced cloak and diamond be-decked hat, a laughing, careless fellow, was best received, men and lads crowding and elbowing one another to get a glimpse of him. Conscious of the popular admiration, fully enjoying it, he stood, for a moment, on the door steps before the open door and framed in a square of yellow candle light, then, with a careless gesture, flung a handful of money to the crowd. His reception contrasted greatly with that accorded to the Duke of Ormond, who, because of his high-handed doings in Ireland, was far from being a favorite, although the story of his evil doing was far greater than the evil itself. Following hard on the Lord Lieutenant was the blind Duke of St. Alban's, who, because of his gout, had to be carried by four footmen to the card table, and, because of his blindness, was accompanied by a companion to tell him the cards.

No sooner had the door closed upon the blind gambler and his attendants, than another chair appeared. Walking before it was a watchman with lantern and staff who had voluntarily constituted himself a kind of herald, shouting as he walked:

"Make way for Colonel Blood! Colonel Blood, my men! Way for the friend of the Irish!"

At that there was excitement and a craning of necks, and, the chair being opened, there stepped forth a slim, active figure of a man dressed in black and silver. On the door step he stood a moment, then, drawing his sword and giving a little flourish of the blade, he bade the pressing crowd stand back.

"A line, my fine fellows! A line!" he called, and made a sweeping motion with his rapier. There was a falling back at once until the space in front of the house was cleared. Then, at a sign, two of his attendants ran swiftly along the pavement stoopingly, one to the right and one to the left, and, as each went, he scattered small coins, much as a housewife scatters chicken feed. All of six yards each way from the door the line was laid, none in the crowd making move until the elegant and dramatic Blood gave a sign. Then a cry went up of "Long live the poor man's friend," and caps were waved. The sword that glittered in the torchlight was sheathed, the crowd scattered to scramble for the coin, and Blood passed out of sight into the house and the door closed behind him.

In the drawing-room Blood was warmly greeted by cavaliers in silk stockings and fine laces, by gaily bedecked ladies with waving plumes and elaborate headdresses, and, here and there, by an army officer. Little groups broke up to welcome him, then re-formed anew with more spirited chattering than before, adding to the confusion of noise. A band of fiddles made music behind a bank of ferns, and in one corner a few laughed loudly at the noisy antics of a gorgeously-dressed young man whom the lookers-on applauded as "Rochester, the imitation mountebank." Avoiding all these, Blood passed through the crowd with occasional smiles and bows and whispered greetings, a man of king-like dignity when he was not consciously posing, one strangely rugged and weather-beaten compared with the rest of the merry-makers, his black and silver dress setting him apart somewhat. So he came, presently, to the room where sat the card players and dice throwers.

"Welcome, fortunate prince. I challenge you to play," called out a diamond-decked lady whose headdress was stuffed with saffron-colored ribbons, as she motioned Blood to a seat at her side.

"If you will forgive me, I would prefer not to play to-night," said Blood with a bow.

"But I have lost, oh, hundreds and hundreds of pounds to-night, and Ormond is unrelenting," wailed the lady.

Ormond, who sat opposite her, dice box in hand, looked up at Blood. He was a man with a fat round face and a quick little eye that looked to drop again, like a flickering fire flame.

"His Grace and I have played before," said Blood. "Few win against him, I am told. Yet, I think that he cannot win always. News has reached me of a certain wager recently made, and that, I think, he may not win." There was a veiled sarcasm in the words and it did not escape Ormond. A frown shot over his face.

"What mean you?" he asked. "I know of no wager."

"Then you will pardon me if I am in error," said Blood. "It is said that you wagered something in relation to a garniture of some kind, a collar, I believe, that you were to wear."

Hearing that, Ormond wrinkled his brow in a puzzled frown and a purple flush touched his cheeks. He checked an impulse to say something, but his attention was called to the game as the lady placed a heap of gold on the table and said, "It is my last."

The box was shaken and the dice rattled out. The woman's face fell as she saw the result of the throw, and the long talons of Ormond's hand swept the new pile of gold to his side of the table. His opponent, fired with the gaming madness, slipped off her rings, her bracelets, her chain, and unfastened a diamond clasp. Against that, the Duke laid the two heaps of gold. Again he won. The lady, with pale and drawn face, her fingers clutching nervously, rose from the table.

Seeing her agitation, Blood said: "Doubtless, the Duke will present Lady Castle with her ring."

"Doubtless," said Ormond in a steely voice, "the gentleman who knows so much of my affairs, will be willing to redeem the ring in a hazard," and a crafty look came into his eyes.

"It was a gift from His Majesty," whispered the lady to Blood.

"I fear that I have not enough to set against so precious a toy," said Blood to Ormond, "but gladly will I set all that I have on a single venture." So saying, he laid upon the table such gold as he had and added a couple of rings and a diamond buckle.

"It is too low a stake to set against a king's gift," said Ormond.

"If you will accept what I have," whispered Buckingham, who had drawn near, "it is gladly yours." He slipped a purse into Blood's hand as he spoke. The man in black and silver courteously acknowledged the favor and poured the contents of the purse in a glittering shower onto the table.

"And again," said Blood, "lest the Duke of Ormond insist upon the full value of the ring, for a king's gift is not to be lightly weighed, permit me to add another trinket, the which I gained but recently from a man I deem of poor spirit." At that, Blood added to the sparkling heap on the table both the diamond hat clasp and the gold chain which, a few hours before, had been the property of the Duke. The Duke stared at chain and clasp with fixed eyes, then, with a start, looked up at Blood, who seemed perfectly unconcerned. Pretending to misunderstand Ormond's look, he said:

"Still barely enough, I admit, to ransom a king's gift to a lady, but it is all that I have here."

Ormond was thunderstruck. He gasped. It was with an effort of will that he prevented himself from shouting out the details of the robbery at Edgeware. Still, as he swiftly reflected, there was no way to connect the gallant before him with the importunate highwayman. So, hoarsely, he said:

"Enough. Let us play. The highest throw gains all," and placed the ring on the table.

Very distinctly then, and with quiet emphasis, Blood said:

"For your promptitude, my lord Duke, many thanks, for my business is of a kind that will hardly endure waiting."

The words came to Ormond as a direct challenge. Well he remembered the parting speech of the highwayman only a few hours ago.

"But gentlemen have no business," said the Duke.

"True," said the imperturbable Blood. "But my affair is in connection with a certain rare collar which you are to wear. You may have forgotten that, my lord, in your attention to the play."

"'Od's blood! Have a care," growled Ormond. "You talk in enigmas and I like them not. I begin to think—" he broke off suddenly.

"It delights me that your Grace remembers," said Blood. "The collar shall be perfectly fitted." He smiled and rattled the dice box as he spoke. Throwing, he saw at a glance that his cast was of no value and a sigh went up from the little knot gathered about the players. Ormond cast, with the result that he swept the money and jewelry over to his side of the table.

Blood bowed and passed among the crowd. To Lady Castle he whispered, "With good fortune I may yet redeem the ring and you shall wear it to-morrow."

A little later he left the house.

—3—

The road to Windsor which the Duke of Ormond had to take that night led along Oxford Street and past Tyburn. A little alarmed at recent happenings, and extra cautious, he had seen to it that his carriage was well guarded. Ahead rode a couple of armed men, in the rear two more, and a guard was beside the driver armed with a pistol. The roads were good and rang hard because of a sharp frost, and the four animals that drew the coach were mettlesome beasts.

At the King's Head Inn there was a stopping for refreshments and it took some time to awaken the innkeeper, who came to the door growling, but, seeing the cavalcade, was all bows immediately, doffing his night cap and offering the hospitality of the house. The sight of the inn room, glowing with the color and light of a blazing fire, the red-curtained windows and pewter-hung walls, these sorely tempted the guards, for the frosty night air had sharpened their appetites even in that short ride from near Tower Hill, and it was a long way to Teddington, where they would stop for the night. So there was a dismounting and a calling for warm drink, and, presently, one of the soldiers bethought him how good a fried mutton chop would taste, and mentioned it to his companions.

That led to a searching for the cook and a routing out of bed of the kitchen boy, and, in a short while, a great frying pan was on the fire and the booted and spurred men were seated about the fireplace, to the great detriment of the man of the kitchen, while the meat sizzled merrily and invited the hungry fellows.

The Duke, in the meantime, paced to and fro over the sanded floor, impatient, but hiding his impatience, knowing full well the advisability of keeping his men in good humor. He called for drink for one and all, though taking none himself, and, all unknown to them, looked to it sharply that no more was brought than they could stand with clear heads. Still, the noise that they made was enough for a pack of roisterers, with their laughing and joking and shouting. The racket indeed disturbed a watch dog in the courtyard, which set up a furious barking.

Attracted by the dog's noise, Ormond went to the door and opened it, to hear, above the barking, the clatter of hoofs and the snorting of a horse. Curious to learn what was afoot he passed out, and, closing the door behind him, walked silently to a corner of the house from the shadow of which he could command a view of the yard. By the flicker of a dying fire in an iron brazier which stood in the center of the court, he saw a man dressed in black and silver, standing by his horse and stuffing things in the saddle bag preparatory to mounting. At that, Ormond loosed his sword in its scabbard and was minded to run on the man, but he hesitated a moment too long, for, with cat-like agility, Blood leaped on his mare and cantered out of the yard.

Then Ormond did things swiftly. There was no time for the preparation of the carriage, nor would pursuit in the lumbering vehicle have been of avail. He seized on the first horse to hand, and, in a mighty roar, called to his men within:

"To horse! Follow me, and ten gold pieces to the first who reaches me."

So he was off, yo-hoing and hallooing like a huntsman with his hounds, his skin a-tingle with the joy of the chase. As for his men, hearing him shout, they came running, hostlers and inn-keeper with them, and even the cook, carrying the pan of frying meat in his hand. A scurrying to horse and a tightening of girths, and much tumult there was then, with a great stir of changing horses that all might ride, and still more confusion in the running back and forth to get cloaks, to pull on boots and to buckle on swords; so much good time flew.

Ormond was no poltroon and hot was his pursuit. Blood, guessing how things were in the inn with the men, turned in his saddle and challenged his pursuer, taunting him, daring him, for before they had gone a quarter of a mile, scarce a few yards separated them.

At a toll there was no time to lose, and Blood's splendid mare rose to it, sailing over the gate like a bird, nor was the hunter that Ormond rode one whit less clever. The spirit of the chase filled both hunter and hunted with a great joy. Faster went the chase, things leaping out of the dark to meet them, now a black little farmhouse where the ringing hoofs awoke dogs and barnyard fowls, again a slow cart on the way to London market; little thatched houses, ragged hedges, fantastic trees whose naked branches were like threatening claws; a stone bridge dangerous with thin ice; the inn at the corner of Edgeware road; then, of a sudden, the gallows at Tyburn, naked black.

Both men drew rein and each laid hand on his sword hilt.

"Here," said Blood, "is the place where we decide the wager. Let us get to work quickly, to the end that we may be finished before the varlets we left at the inn come upon us."

Ormond made no answer and both men leaped lightly to the ground, cast their horses' reins loose and fell on guard.

"A moment," said the gallant Ormond. "The ring that was Lady Castle's is about my neck should you be the victor, but there is small need that you should know, seeing that I have a mind that it shall stay there."

Blood laughed. "I hope to take it off, my lord, to make place for that other collar of which we spoke."

Then swords were crossed and they fell to work. Ormond had the greater weight and strength of wrist and attacked Blood furiously. But Blood was quick and light in his movements, bounding nimbly from side to side as the other thrust. Neither man escaped bloodletting, though there was nothing of any seriousness. By a dexterous move, a crouching and a leaping sideways, Blood forced the position so that Ormond's back was to the scaffold. Evade and thrust as he might, Ormond was steadily driven backwards, so it befell that soon he set foot on the steps which led to the gallows platform and thus had the advantage of height. A swift thrust on the part of Ormond and the point of his blade passed through Blood's left shoulder. For a

Ormond lay on the scaffold floor, his arms bound, and the hangman's rope about his neck

moment, the highwayman's peril was extreme. But in less than a couple of seconds the tables were turned. Snake-like, Blood's lithe blade seemed to wrap itself about that of Ormond; then a quick turn of the wrist and the Duke's sword went flying, to fall clattering on the hard earth.

Like an angry lion Ormond roared, his brow clouded, and he laid a hand on his dagger. Seeing that, Blood dropped the point of his sword. At that instant there came faintly to the men's ears the distant clatter of hoofs. It was plain to Blood that in a very short while he must be overpowered by numbers, and, like a hound, he leaped at his opponent. Ormond, surprised at the onset, stumbled against the steps. Then the sinewy arms of Blood seized and held him and they fought like a pair of wildcats, forgetful of chivalry, forgetful of everything. Wild wrestling and much rough-and-tumble work were there then, but, when the tip of the pale sun shot its first shaft of cold light, Ormond lay on the scaffold floor, his arms bound, and the hangman's rope about his neck.

Blood hastily possessed himself of the ring, and, with the sound of furious shouting in his ears, leaped down the steps, mounted his mare, fastened the bridle of Ormond's horse to his saddle and was out of sight before the men-at-arms found their lord trussed and fuming with anger, on the scaffold floor.

(December 6th, 1670.)

BLOOD'S GREAT THEFT

—1—

WHEN Bartholomew Fair was in full swing, it was a something by no means to be missed, for, on a day when the May sun shone warm and was cooled by a soft west breeze, there were few, high or low, rich or poor, who did not go there. Queens have played rustic in such places, and duchesses have mimed as orange girls. For it was the great London event, next in importance to Lord Mayor's Day, and neither plague nor fire had put an end to it. All and sundry attended the fair, dashing young fellows from Court, fashionable and gayly dressed ladies and those who wore leather. There were lads with cudgels ready for game or for fight; girls with gay ribbons and cheap finery; watchmen and soldiers; lean dogs sniffing and growling; leather-aproned workmen with sleeves rolled up on brawny arms, who had stolen an hour from the workshop; bagpipe players and drummers; men who had performing bears; thieves who plied their trade under the very eyes of the watch; fellows who had been wounded in the wars and displayed their hurts; vendors of sweets and cakes; there gathered, indeed, at Bartholomew Fair, a sample of living London, a something as representative as the contents of a trawling net that reveals the life of the water in which it has been cast.

Lady Castle had left her coach, and, with a companion, one well known at Court, had enjoyed to the full what was there to enjoy, even partaking of the roasted pig cooked for all comers, and the cakes provided by a city company for the crowd. She had visited the booth where the Irish giant exhibited himself, had talked with him and marveled when his inches were marked against the wall by attendants all chosen for their low stature in order that the greatness of the giant might appear to the better advantage. Other things, too, she had seen, the man who climbed outside a church steeple; the strong man of Topham who bent nails with his teeth and rolled pewter plates with his fingers; the puppet play, most popular attraction there; the Punch and Judy show; the pig-faced lady, and that strange animal recently brought from Africa called a baboon. So, for a while, she walked and laughed with my Lord Shaftesbury, who, like a boy, had loaded himself with things bought, with toys and trinkets, and, tiring of that, had been for a while a popular hero, standing on an upturned tub and casting his purchases high in the air for people to scramble for, laughing heartily to see folk coming at a jog trot in the hope of getting something for nothing.

While standing on the edge of the crowd, Lady Castle had been saluted by a man in a fine, sky-blue coat splendidly laced, whom she had met before somewhere but whose name she did not at first recall. But he introduced himself as Samuel Pepys and seemed highly delighted to be in her company, so with him she walked awhile, rather enjoying his keen delight in the fair than the fair itself, of which she had commenced to tire. At last she told her companion to take her to her coach, which he proceeded to do, but on the way, there were many sad delays. For Mr. Pepys was one of those happily curious folk, who must see everything. If he chanced to hear a child sing prettily, then he must stop to listen. A countryman carrying a large goose was, to him, something of vast interest and he had to question the countryman. Where did he live? and did he find the town to his liking? Then, too, passing the booth in which the strong man of Topham performed, Mr. Pepys had to stop, that he might secure a piece of pewter rolled by the man. At the giant's place nothing would do but that he must climb on a stool and verify, with his own measurement, the giant's height. And, when at last, my lady tossed her head petulantly, saying that if Mr. Pepys was more interested in the fair than in her company he might leave her, he was all humiliation, begging her to go with him to one more booth, where, said he, "is to be seen the most wonderful thing of all, and one which it did indeed do my heart good to see."

So she went with him to the farther side of the fair grounds where they saw a long and low building, on the outside of which stood a trumpeter who called on the people to enter and behold the most wonderful swordsman in the three kingdoms. They entered together and took a seat on a bench, two in a little crowd that sat in front of a candle-lighted platform, and very soon there appeared on the stage a lithe fellow who announced himself to be Jacob Hall.

For a short while he stood, grinning triumphantly and now and then bowing, until a man stood up before the sight-seers, a stout fellow with a red beard, who carried, for show, a great battle-ax, and after stamping for silence, bawled with deafening violence that the man on the platform was, indeed, none other than Jacob Hall, sword servant to his Majesty King Charles II, and, as such, challenged any man in the world to do the things that he did. The speech being finished, there was a flourish on a trumpet, the people stamped their feet and knocked sticks on the benches, and Jacob Hall commenced to throw himself about the stage, turning flip flaps and somersets, leaping over two barrels stood on end and doing other things most extraordinary, to the immense delight of Master Pepys, who, in his eagerness, had left Lady Castle and pressed close to the platform the better to see, his eyesight, as he explained to the lady, not being as keen as once it had been.

It was all stupendously effective, that leaping and twisting and turning, and there went about the seats a kind of whispered commentary, something like the intermezzo of whispers that a musician is conscious of between two movements of a number played. But all applause was checked when four men marched on to the stage, each with a sword. The four knelt in a square with sword points sticking upright. Jacob Hall posed awhile, conveying the impression that the proposed task was too dangerous a one to attempt, then, excitement being at the proper pitch, he ran to the farther end of the platform, launched himself forward and, as a hurdler flies over the hurdles, leaped over the swords. There were shouts of delight and much applause, and, catching the eye of her escort and beckoning to him, Lady Castle made to leave the place. She was halted before she had gone three steps, for, from the rear of the hall came a challenge.

"Well done and bravely done," said a voice. "I challenge Jacob Hall to match me in skill or in strength."

Lady Castle turned with a start, saw the challenger, and, for a moment, they regarded one another. She saw him, a well-built, active man, slender as a harrier, clad in soft brown, close-fitting garments, and knew him at once for Colonel Thomas Blood. There was the promise of a smile on her lips, but her heart was heavy. It came to her with a shock of pain that he had dared too much in venturing where a reward was offered for his capture because of the Ormond affair. But beyond the first glance of recognition he took no further notice of her, climbing over the seats, passing through a gap made by the spectators as they bent this way and that, leaping lightly onto the stage. There he threw off his cloak, casting it carelessly to whomsoever chanced to catch it, the lucky one being the delighted Samuel Pepys.

No matter how much Lady Castle wished to leave then, nothing would have moved her, though she trembled for the personal safety of her friend and cousin.

"My sword against the sword of Jacob Hall!" said Blood. "Or I will wrestle with him or leap with him. It is his to choose which. For I hold that a man who has lived in Ireland has that in his bones which no Englishman can better."

That little boastful speech set up a hubbub. What Hall might have chosen, wished to choose, had no weight. The audience settled the matter. Cries went up of "A challenge! A challenge!" and were heard by those outside, so others came pouring in until the place was crowded. "A wrestling match!" came from one stout-lunged fellow, and the cry became general.

Meanwhile, Hall and his unknown opponent had prepared themselves and were stripped and belted. For full a minute the two circled about, each with his right hand on the left shoulder of the other, each left hand cupping the right elbow of his opponent in the English fashion, neither at first willing to irritate his man. Then, as by a single thought, both men grappled, battling rough and strong, and swift and short was the work. There was a mighty straining, a moment of doubt, and the locked pair went down, rolling over and over, twisting and turning, smashing down the candles in their fall so that the place was in semi-darkness in a moment. Some one picked up the only candle remaining alight and attempted to relight the other candles, but, coming too near to the wrestlers, was knocked down.

It was a poor end to a brave beginning, for, not liking the semi-darkness, the spectators rapidly forsook the place, the more as some rival attraction outside sounded a drum and pan pipes, and, by the time the room was again lighted, the hall was empty of all but a half-dozen, and a little group was near the stage, made up of Lady Castle, Pepys, Jacob Hall and his unknown challenger. The King's swordsman walked a little lame and he was somewhat grim of face, but, like a true man, he took his defeat and held out a hand to his opponent telling him that he was the better man.

"And," said he, "doubtless you will give me a chance to prove myself."

"That will I, and soon," said Blood heartily. "Belike before twenty-four hours have passed, for now that I know your mettle, I am well content."

So he took his cloak from Pepys and threw it about him, and, with a bow, offered Lady Castle his arm.

—2—

Outside, Lady Castle directed her steps towards the place where her coach was waiting, and, after a few steps, thanked and dismissed Mr. Pepys. To Blood she said, as they walked:

"Now what, in the name of all the saints, do you here and in that guise? Are you not aware that a reward is offered for your capture because of the affair at Tyburn, Cousin?"

Thomas Blood waved his hand airily, then threw his cloak over his shoulder with a flourish as he said: "I am well aware. But far less fearful now than when I dared to enter London to return to you the ring that I took from Ormond."

"But the danger—" she said.

"I have been well warned," he answered. "Be that as it may, my life and my fortunes are with Ireland. There were those whom England robbed, there were those made poor by Cromwell's men, and where England robbed, there must England pay."

"I do not understand your riddles. What have you to do with England's paying back that which she robbed?"

"Hear me," commanded Blood, and paused in his walk. It was a place free of people and they could talk in comfort, though still the lady was ill at ease because of the number of her friends there who knew Blood. "When I rendered you a slight service in the matter of the King's ring, you promised to aid me. Now it is that I call on you to do me a service."

She said nothing, but lifted her hand and showed him the ring on her finger.

"To-day," he continued, "I was in the room in the Tower where the regalia is kept, and I saw the crown jewels, things brave with gold and jewels—the orb, the scepter, the crown itself—and it came to me that the brightest ruby in the crown should be yours. Not only that, but I thought that the worth of all that stuff should be given to those in Ireland whom England made poor in her wars."

"Riddles again," half whispered the lady, a fear at her heart.

"No riddle, cousin," declared Blood. "I will take the crown jewels from where they are and deliver them to the diamond merchants of Amsterdam in Holland, and the money that the trumpery brings I shall scatter among the poor in Ireland, under the nose of the Lord Lieutenant. No riddle is there."

Hearing that, the lady stood amazed. "What madness is this?" she asked. "It is madder than the affair at Tyburn. It is madder than your playing highwayman."

Blood went on, not heeding her, talking almost as one in a dream. "The guard in the Tower room is this same Jacob Hall, and to-day, hearing that he was at Bartholomew Fair, I came to try his mettle, to meet him face to face so that I might know what kind of fellow it is that I must tussle with."

"But what part have I in all this?"

"To-morrow, meet me at the Tower drawbridge, plainly dressed, for I must lose no time."

"But it is mad," she protested.

"All will fall out well," insisted Blood. "My stars are with me. Be there at ten and look for me in some disguise, though what, I do not yet know."

And having arrived at the place, the amazing man handed Lady Castle into her coach, strode off and was lost in the crowd.

—3—

Lady Castle was at the bridgehead, at the appointed place and at the specified time, and picked out Blood easily. He was talking to one of the beef-eaters, as the men of the Tower were popularly called, and dressed as a clergyman. Having gone past the initial stage, she knew that there was little more before her than to carry out her part to the best advantage, though she seemed to have been swept into the affair as a leaf is swept by the summer breeze. The churchly-looking man in black saluted her gravely, offered her his arm, and together they walked down the gravel path, stood for a moment, to disarm suspicion, at the Traitor's Gate, then went on towards the Tower where the crown jewels are kept.

"You have to do little, to say little, and only to follow the plans I make, and the plans are—"

"Yes. At least tell me that," she said eagerly.

"The plans are not yet made," he added gravely.

"But how—"

"It must be much as we played charades when we

were children, the one following the lead of the other as things come to pass. But say no more, for churchly men do not chatter, and you see the character I have adopted."

And so the wonderful adventure started.

At the Tower Gate they were met by the chief keeper of the jewels, a man named Edwards, and he was attended by the doughty Jacob Hall as guard. What the keeper and his assistant guard saw, was a slimly built clergyman with a lady whom they took to be his wife, so Edwards was all politeness at once and dismissed Hall to smoke at his will, until he should be required.

In character with his appearance, Blood made some remark about the transient value of gold and precious stones, and Mr. Edwards, accustomed to hear expressions of wonder and of admiration from his visitors, was a little piqued at finding his treasures slighted. He went to lengths to display the regalia to the best advantage. He lifted the crown from its cushion and held it to the light, calling on his visitors to note the flashing jewels and the rich decorations. From cases he brought out other wonders, great gold goblets, immense plates richly chased, wonderfully ornamented dishes set with precious stones—regal symbols that bore rubies, amethysts, diamonds, sapphires, great glorious pearls and emeralds. It excited him to further display that he could arouse the visitors to no enthusiasm.

"Treasures that are no treasures," said Blood, gently, as Hall, at the word of Edwards, brought to him for his admiration a new and splendid dish of gold that was a present for Nell Gwynn. "Far greater than all those treasures is the treasure that I have here." He turned and bowed at Lady Castle as he spoke, then, with an exclamation of alarm, said, "But what ails you?"

Hearing that, both Edwards and Hall became concerned. The keeper of the jewels suspected faintness, and sent Hall for water.

"It is but a fainting spell, a sudden weakness," said Blood. "I greatly fear that the sight of so much unaccustomed glitter has been too much. Sometimes at Court—" He stopped suddenly as one who was on the verge of talking too freely.

But Mr. Edwards pricked up his ears at the mention of Court, and there arose in his mind a vision of a minister's wife, modest and retiring, soberly dressed and quiet of mien, moving in the midst of powdered and perfumed beauties of high estate, a gentle creature of aristocratic refinement in illustrious society. That the lady had dealings of an intimate nature with the great and powerful was to him evident, and his inner self began to build projects, to dwell on possible preferment. An expression of intense commiseration came over his countenance as the lady, led by Blood, walked with feeble steps to the door, her head bent to catch the whispers of the gentle churchman.

Suddenly, the sympathy of Edwards overcame his discretion. Would the lady deign to accept the hospitality of his dwelling? Would she permit his wife and daughter to minister to her until the fainting spell had passed away?

Hearing that, Blood was full of gratitude. "If," said he, "you would be so kind," and bowed with courtly grace to Edwards, at the same time gently drawing the lady aside so that the jewel-keeper might show the way.

"It is very kind of you," murmured the lady. "Already I feel revived. This faintness will soon pass." She took a step and the gallant keeper of the jewels sprang forward, noticing her evident weakness. "Do not mind me," she said. "It is dreadful that I should be overcome at a moment when you were preparing your sermon, the sermon on which so much was to hang. His Majesty—"

"Hush!" said Blood. Then turning to Edwards, he whispered: "My text was to have been on the Vanity of Riches. The true delight of solitary study and of temperate pleasure I had it in mind to emphasize. But perhaps it does not so greatly matter," and a heavy sigh escaped him.

"And Lord Shaftesbury. In less than an hour he will be at our house," said the lady, very disconsolate.

"If you will but allow me," said Edwards brightly, "I will make a suggestion. Rest awhile in my house. My wife will attend you, and my coach shall be immediately prepared. May I have the honor to escort you? Is it too much that I ask? Am I officious?"

"On the contrary," said Blood gravely. "But if I

am to stay here, I must be well assured that the lady will leave before half an hour. There is an appointment—"

"It shall be as you say," said Edwards.

A moment of doubt seemed to assail Blood, and he said:

"But I fear it is better that we let the matter of the sermon go. Your duty as jewel-keeper prevents your absence, and I am no fit man to stand guard over so much, nor no fighter of brawn and muscle to oppose thieves who might break in and steal."

The keeper of the jewels gave a little laugh at this.

"Thieves do not dare to steal here," he said. "And there is the stout Jacob Hall who is on guard, a man of mettle and great bravery, and swordsman to the King."

Hearing that, the lady put her hand to her heart. She was, she said, relieved. The sermon on the Vanity of Riches would be preached for the King, and she would soon recover with a little rest. As for the promise of the coach, that mended matters so that Lord Shaftesbury would not be incommoded. As for his reverence, having seen his fill of the jewels, he could follow at his leisure. And Mr. Edwards and his wife must give her the opportunity to thank them, for such kindness should by no means go unrewarded.

"But see to it," urged Blood, "that you leave the Tower before a half hour is gone—"

So on the arm of Mr. Edwards, the lady passed down

the steps and out of the place, and Blood was left alone in the jewel room to ponder and to moralize. A minute later Jacob Hall reëntered and took his place as guard.

—4—

The treasure room was a stone chamber at the top of a tower, and the only approach to it was a narrow, winding flight of steps. The place in which the regalia was kept was lighted by some half-a-dozen high, narrow windows. A heavy, nail-studded oak door stood half open, at the head of the steps.

At the door, Jacob Hall looked into the chamber and saw the clergyman, a spare built man in black, standing with his back to a window, his arms folded, gazing, as if only half seeing the treasure. Neither spoke, and the silence was broken only by the twittering of birds heard through a narrowly opened window. Jacob Hall walked slowly around the treasure chamber, then took a seat upon an iron-bound chest that stood on the side of the chamber farthest from Blood and a few yards from the door. He was careful to make no noise, so as to leave the meditating man undisturbed. Blood watched him with a careless eye and with a detached kind of interest. Then, suddenly and swiftly, he strode to the door, slammed it shut and turned the great key in the lock. At that, Hall sprang up eagerly, astonished. In another moment Blood had stripped off his black coat and stood, a tall, white-haired man. Then off went wig and tie and Hall recognized his opponent at the Fair the day before.

"What fool's trick is this?" cried Hall, peevishly. "This is neither time nor place for a wrestling match though you did beat me yesterday."

"We must make it both time and place," said Blood. "There is much to do."

Hall's mind worked painfully for a second, then it came to him that there was more in the other's actions than he had imagined.

"What is your mission?" he asked, and as he spoke, he edged a little to the right. Suddenly stretching out his arm he seized a halberd that stood in a rack with other weapons, and, bringing it to a level, made a pass at Blood. Blood was swift as a hare, leaping to one side, neatly dodging the cutting edge and seizing the pole in his right hand. For an instant Hall held fast to his end, held, indeed, until he saw that the struggle had become a mere tug-of-war, when he released his hold and darted at Blood. Fierce and heavy was his attack, so much so that in the impact Blood was borne backwards, almost lost his balance, and was saved from falling by stumbling against a heavy stand, on which rested some plate. Both men locked, wrestled and swayed, while gold plate went clattering to the stone floor. There was a nervous alacrity about Blood that offset Hall's superior weight and the struggle for mastery was tremendous. Around and about they twisted and turned, each trying to get a grip of the other's throat, each cautiously defensive. Then both went down with a crash, tripped by the long handle of the halberd that lay on the floor. Hall was on his feet first, and, with a grunt, flung himself at Blood, at a moment when the latter had turned over, quick as a lizard, and was on his hands and knees. So, missing his mark, Hall stumbled over the kneeling Blood and went down like a felled ox. The fall knocked the breath out of his body and before he could recover, Blood was on top of him, sitting astride of his chest. But the stout swordsman was too dazed to make any further resistance just then. He lay, panting heavily, his eyes staring up at his opponent.

Certainly it was a strange use for a queen's embroidered scarf, but Blood that day used one as a gag for a man. Further, he took another embroidered silken piece, twisted it into a kind of rope and tied Hall hand and foot. By the time he had finished, the King's swordsman came to his senses and saw what followed, but with no power to prevent.

Blood took the crown, held it up for a moment, turning it in the sunlight to enjoy the flashing light from a hundred gems, then bundled it in a cloth of silk. The orb he placed in another cloth. For a moment he weighed the probabilities of having time to file the scepter in two and take that, for as it was, it was too long and unwieldy, but he abandoned the idea. Going to a cabinet where lay the precious stones to be used in the ornamentation of other kingly things, he poured the glittering jewels into a small leather pouch. The bundles containing the crown and orb he hung about his shoulders, then, taking a long blue cloak from an open press, he threw it over all. As a last precaution he added a large pistol which hung near the rack from which the halberd had been taken, looking well to the priming.

Seeing all this, Hall looked so sad, yet so helpless, that Blood held out a hand to him, laughing.

"The disguise will carry me through, friend Hall, though sorry I am that you may not be abroad to see, but must remain here trussed. I have gone a-mumming before this, many's the time. But have no grief that you are vanquished, for it is Colonel Thomas Blood before whom you fell—the same who stopped the coach of Ormond, who placed a hemp collar about the neck of the Lord Lieutenant of Ireland. So farewell. I must lock the door on you and begone, and the quicker, the less time for discovery."

For a couple of seconds Blood stood in the doorway listening, then, hearing no sound, he slammed the door and locked it, pitching the key out of a window. He reached the drawbridge without incident. There, at the outer end, he had the ill luck to be challenged by a young halberdier, one new to the business and keen, a little suspicious of the bulging cloak. At his challenge, a companion at arms came running.

It was manifestly clear to Blood that his getting out, at such a rate, was likely to be a much more lengthy business than he had anticipated. To his alarm, too, he saw, a little way off, Edwards coming at a run, probably attracted by the disturbance at the bridge. Clearly, no time was to lose. He surveyed the situation at a glance, then, realizing the gravity of it, drew his pistol and fired at the first halberdier. The fellow fell to the ground and Blood threw away the pistol and picked up the halberd. With it he met the second man, parried his thrust and ran him through the leg. Blood turned, to see Edwards almost upon him, and the same glance showed him that Lady Castle, by some means which he did not try to guess, had gotten outside the Tower and was entering a coach. Across the grass plot then he fled, his stolen crown and his orb banging his ribs sorely, his cloak a-flutter in the wind, itself an encumbrance. For a moment he thought of flight riverwards, next of a dash for London Bridge, but fearing interference, he turned towards Tower Hill where the way was clear. Straight for the low wall he went, taking a leap that might have hurt him badly had he not lighted on a newly-dug flower bed. Half-a-dozen yards off was a butcher's horse, the butcher's lad being but a short distance away. To that sped Blood and a moment later was in the saddle, kicking the beast vigorously.

Blood's stars were against him. Suddenly, coming from the direction of the city, appeared Captain Beckman and two horse soldiers, and to them Edwards called lustily, the men-at-arms joining in the cry. The three horsemen took in at a glance that something untoward was afoot, and, seeing the flying horseman, clapped heels to their horses in pursuit. A lucky shot from Beckman's pistol brought Blood's horse down and, in falling, the crown broke loose and rolled in the roadway, jewels dropping from it as it bumped on the cobblestones. Leaving the crown to its fate, Blood cast off the hampering cloak and took to his heels, but the three horsemen were hot on his trail and at the top of Tower Hill they overtook him.

The pursued man ran to a low wall, against which he stood, facing his pursuers, somewhat of a commanding figure in spite of his plight, hatless, cloakless and combat stained.

A little crowd gathered then and Blood stepped forward, brushing aside a soldier who would have laid hands on him, and addressing Captain Beckman, said: "My life is now in your hands. Order one of your fellows to give me a horse, and I will ride unattended, or with you as a gentleman, to the Tower." Then he stood, looking about him with great unconcern.

There were murmurs of approval among the bystanders, and one stout fellow in a leathern apron pressed forward, hotly shouting that Blood should not be taken, but Blood waved him back with a gesture. Beckman made a sign with his hand, and a trooper dismounted and held his horse for Blood to mount, and five minutes later officer and prisoner rode side by side across the drawbridge into the Tower, and the portcullis fell in the face of the noisy crowd.

—5—

On that same day, the King was in St. James' Park, feeding his ducks. He was a swarthy-faced fellow, all of five-foot ten inches high, with a deep bass voice, and his loud, boisterous laugh belied his frowning countenance. When he saw his attendant, the Duke of Leeds, coming in haste, he uttered a word of warning. " 'Od's fish!" said he. "Slowly, man, slowly, or you will frighten my ducks."

"I beg your Majesty's pardon," began my lord, but the King interrupted him at once, not without an oath, telling him that affairs of state could not be so pressing but that he must be interrupted when he was at play. But my lord was insistent, blurting out that some one had tried to rob him of his crown. So the King sounded a note of incredulity, whereupon the courtier had his opportunity, and, having regained his breath, told the amazing story. Then, to the thinking of the Duke and the other courtiers, things became preposterous, for the King burst out into a fit of noisy laughter.

"Morbleu, my lord Duke," said he as soon as he could control himself, "the rascal must be such a fellow as I have been looking for. Set a thief to catch a thief. What better man could I have than one who so desires the crown that he will see to it that none other steals it? Why, my lord Duke, he is a better man than you. You pity me because he would steal the crown and he envies me for having it, and it is better to be envied than pitied." Pleased with his own conceit, he went off into another fit of laughter.

"Has your majesty no orders, then?" asked the Duke.

" 'Od's fish, yes!" said the King. "See that the fellow is brought to Whitehall. He is either a God Almighty's fool or a brave man who takes my crown. If he is the first, the Tower is no place for him, and if he is the second, then we want him about us."

That night, in Whitehall, Colonel Blood stood before the King and told his tale, nor was it a short one, for the King desired to know full particulars, and when the merry monarch heard the story of the defeat of Jacob Hall, he was in ecstasies of delight.

"A hard morsel for my Lady Castlemaine to swallow," said he, and again laughed noisily. "For," he added, "little Castlemaine holds that of all men in England there is none to match Jacob Hall."

After awhile, the King became serious, yet watching him closely, Blood could see nothing in his manner of rigid disapproval. When he spoke again it was with something akin to a roar.

"Have you nothing to ask for? No pardon? No favor?"

"Never have I asked a favor, your Majesty," replied Blood. "I may steal, but not beg."

"A troublesome subject," said the King. "In my Worcester days I found many such."

There was another long pause, then, suddenly, his face lighted to a rare smile and he slapped his knee in high good humor.

"You seem to have done amazingly well," he said, "on nothing a year. Let us see what kind of guardian for our person you are on a pension. By God's Death, on three hundred pounds a year you should be able to refrain from trying to hang my Lord Lieutenant, or beating Jacob Hall, or stealing the crown jewels. Eh, fellow?"

Evidently Blood was of the same mind, for he found nothing to say contrary to the amazing sentence and enjoyed both his pension and the King's favor until August 24th, 1680, the day of his death.

JACK SHEPPARD

Highwayman and Prison-Breaker

SAINT GILES'S BOWL

I

Where Saint Giles's church stands, once a lazar-house stood;
And chain'd to its gates was a vessel of wood;
A broad-bottom'd bowl from which all the fine fellows,
Who pass'd by that spot, on their way to the gallows,
   Might tipple strong beer
   Their spirits to cheer,
 And drown in a sea of good liquor, all fear!
 And nothing the transit to Tyburn beguiles
 So well as a draught from the bowl of Saint Giles!

II

By many a highwayman many a draught
Of nutty-brown ale at St. Giles's was quaft,
Until the old lazar-house chanced to fall down,
And the broad-bottom'd bowl was removed to the Crown.
   Where the robber may cheer,
   His spirit with beer,
 And drown in a sea of good liquor all fear!
 For nothing the transit to Tyburn beguiles
 So well as a draught from the bowl of Saint Giles!

III

There Mulsack and Swiftneck, both prigs from their birth,
Old Mob and Tom Cox, took their last draught on earth:
There Randal, and Shorter, and Whitney pull'd up,
And jolly Jack Joyce drank his finishing cup!
   For a can of ale calms
   A highwayman's qualms,
 And makes him sing blithely his dolorous psalms!
 And nothing the transit to Tyburn beguiles
 So well as a draught from the bowl of Saint Giles!

IV

When gallant Tom Sheppard to Tyburn was led,—
"Stop the cart at the Crown—stop a moment," he said.
He was offered the Bowl, but he left it and smiled,
Crying, "Keep it till call'd for by Jonathan Wild!
       "The rascal one day
       "Will pass by this way,
"And drink a full measure to moisten his clay!
"And never will Bowl of St. Giles have beguiled
"Such a thorough-paced scoundrel as JONATHAN WILD!"

V

Should it e'er be my lot to ride backwards that way,
At the door of the Crown I will certainly stay;
I'll summon the landlord—I'll call for the Bowl,
And drink a deep draught to the health of my soul!
       What ever may hap
       I'll taste of the tap,
To keep up my spirits when brought to the crap!
For nothing the transit to Tyburn beguiles
So well as a draught from the Bowl of St. Giles!

JACK SHEPPARD

FROM Willesden to Huntingdon is not far short of a hundred miles as the road winds, but the youngster, Jack Sheppard, started off alone to make the journey one day in June, in the year 1716. A sharp-featured lad he, with a hard bright stare and sallow skin, ignorant as to books and learning, but wise in some of the darker ways of the world. Undersized and underfed, disinclined for work and certainly dishonest, he was looked on with suspicion in his native village of Willesden. Then, too, he was suspiciously fond of London, thinking nothing of a trudge down the Harrow Road until it met Edgeware Road, where he would hang around the Paddington Inn until some town-bound coach drew up for a change of horses, when, by hook or crook, he would gain a ride.

One day the St. Alban's coach brought a man, a brown-faced, grim kind of fellow who chattered like a cock sparrow as the coach passengers sat in the big paneled room, and the fellow had much to say about a woman and her daughter at Huntingdon who had been accused of dealings with the devil, of witchcraft, of casting the evil eye on their neighbors' cattle, and he went on to relate that the pair of them were to be hanged. At that, thirteen-year-old Jack pricked up his ears, for a hanging he had never seen. Men in the pillory and in the stocks, yes, and once he had the rare and glorious experience of seeing a madman in chains, but an execution never. So he held an attentive ear, learned the direction of Huntingdon and the time it might take to go there, and, also, as near as might be, the time when the execution would take place, then set off for Willesden again, walking briskly—as unpromising a boy as could be with his dust-begrimed face, ragged shirt and bramble-torn knee-breeches.

Arrived at Willesden he avoided his home, waiting in an old barn until the crescent moon appeared, when he went quietly by back ways to the village chandler's shop, somehow got in, robbed the till of its money and, feeling that he had well provided himself for the journey, started off. All night he walked under the starlit sky, and when the first light began to appear in the east he encountered a farmer's cart and begged a ride. So, sometimes riding, sometimes walking, he arrived in Huntingdon in good time for the sight he had set out to see, and, pushing somewhat rudely, as a Huntingdon man thought, to get near the scaffold, was soundly cuffed. But for that young Jack cared little, and in after years he made it a boast that in his boyhood he had seen the last judicial execution for witchcraft in England.

And the sight whetted his appetite for more, so that, thereafter, not a public execution did he miss. Thus it came that a couple of years later, at Bunhill row, he had another exceptionally delightful experience when he chanced to be one of a noisy mob viewing the strange spectacle of the hanging of the public hangman, when John Price, who had turned off many a good man, met his doom, and it was there that he became first acquainted with Jonathan Wild. The great thief-taker was pointed out to him by Blueskin, the highwayman, and Jack was at once ablaze with curiosity. That night he went by appointment to the Red Lion Tavern in Billingsgate, where, in a long, low room the walls of which were hung with announcements of executions, notices of rewards for the capture of evil-doers, and ballad sheets, Wild sat at a table with a tankard of ale before him. There were many others there, playing cards or sprawled along the benches around the wall, and Jack found himself something of a notoriety when it was announced that he was the son of Tom Sheppard who had been hanged for highway robbery. This Jack had not hitherto known, but learning, he was filled with pride in his parentage.

Somewhere towards midnight, at the request of Jonathan Wild, young Sheppard gave an exhibition of his dexterity by breaking into the wooden draper's at the corner of Cornhill and Gracechurch Street, and duly carried the spoils to Jonathan Wild. It was an adventure requiring presence of mind and agility, with vulpine sharpness, for the draper slept on the premises and the apprentice had his pallet in the shop itself; but there was successful outcome. So Jonathan Wild bestowed upon Jack one-fourth of what he had taken, and promised him his protection, and the young Sheppard was launched on his life of breezy freedom.

In the silence of the night and the darkness of the morning he plied his trade then for many a day, a remarkably active young man, and, now and then, there was a change from housebreaking, when, with Blueskin, the road to Romford was patrolled. As highwaymen, the pair had some success, especially in the summer of 1720 when business was brisk in Exchange Alley. For that was the year of the South Sea Bubble and people from the countryside flocked to town as "visions of ingots danced before their eyes." Good money for cattle and sheep and pigs sold at Chelmsford or Brentwood was taken to London. Sometimes Sheppard got the money, and sometimes it was lost with swiftness when delivered to some bubble company in return for stock. For of companies in those days there was no end, stock was offered and sold by rogues and citizens of credit and renown equally: stock for trading in human hair: for furnishing funerals in any part of Great Britain: for extracting silver from lead: for lending money on bubble stock: for a machine for perpetual motion: for a company for carrying on an undertaking of great

Jack Sheppard on the road to Tyburn

advantage the details of which were to be kept secret. And so on. At last, Sheppard found business brisker in 'Change Alley and Cornhill than on the Romford Road, for in the city streets from the earliest dawn there was a kind of eddy of people, a human stream where weaklings were crowded aside and stronger ones plunged in; there were men and women in dainty clothes sometimes fighting side by side, struggling like wild things to reach the brokers' offices: in the heat and the dust of crowded streets, thirsty, hungry, tired people stood by the hour and there were arguments and fights and disputes. But rich and poor, gentle or rough, all were supplied with money. And among these Jack Sheppard plied the trade of pickpocket with great success, sometimes indeed making exceptionally good hauls by robbing the treasuries of the company promoters.

An enormous success he was until he became filled with the idea that Jack was as good as his master, and threw security to the winds by refusing to give three-fourths of his harvest to Jonathan Wild.

"What I gets I keeps from now on," said Jack with emphasis, and Wild reflected on the spirit of his words.

"Then," said Wild, ending a long pause, "if you turns against me, I turns against you," and the great alliance was ended then and there. Mr. Wild became resolutely indignant, set his men to work, and that night Jack Sheppard was lodged in Saint Giles's Roundhouse in Kendrick Yard.

It was not much of a prison considered from a modern point of view. It was more like an oddly designed tower of stone with something of the general appearance of a huge barrel two stories in height. Indeed, except for the heavily barred little windows, a stranger to its use might have supposed it some queer warehouse. Sheppard was delivered to the janitor and ordered to be handcuffed, but, there being few prisoners treated in that fashion, the jailer had to make search. While doing so, he left Jack Sheppard in the common room, a kind of hallway. It was not for long that he was so left, but long enough for the ferret-witted fellow to seize his advantage. For, standing in a corner, he saw an old halberd and from it he wrenched the head, which he concealed in his clothing.

When the jailer returned it was without the handcuffs, for the only pair to be found were broken. But calling in an assistant, Master Jack was dragged, not without cuffs and blows, upstairs and into an upper chamber. There his hands were tied with rope, a second rope was passed over his wrists and the two ends fastened to a stone ring, and so he was left.

As soon as Sheppard heard the key turned in the lock, he set to work. It was sufficiently easy to loose the rope from the ring, though his hands were tied, and a little wriggling and straining did the rest, for the jailers had been inexpert in their knottings. Next he attacked the barred window, working with his halberdhead at the mortar, so that in a very short while he had the bars loose. The ropes with which he had been tied afforded a means of escape then, for fastening them together and tying them to the remaining window bars, he had a line that reached almost to the ground. By midnight he was free.

After that, Mr. Sheppard's lines were not cast in pleasant places. He prowled about the old quarters, in the streets near the river side, but with caution, for everywhere were men not to be trusted, men attached one way or another to Jonathan Wild, and a deepening realization of the danger everywhere came upon him. And his evil anticipations were only too well justified, for the thief-taker had cast his nets.

Once more there were, for a little, fairly prosperous times, when, in company with Blueskin, he took to the road and worked the country about Tunbridge Wells. Then, with money, there was London, and Master Jack appeared in the riverside haunts, fashionably dressed in scarlet coat embroidered with gold, ruffled shirt and laced hat. He played the beau in sorry ale houses and made his headquarters in a gambling den behind Wych Street. Money running low, he resumed his nocturnal activities in company with a new acquaintance, Blueskin having fallen into the toils of the law, and a raid was made upon a cutler's shop in Ludgate Street. The plan involved the entry into the house by Sheppard while his partner kept watch, and all went very well until Jack started to make his exit, the booty in his hands. As he bent to crawl out through the little window, he was astonished to see his partner raise a heavy club. He tried to draw back but was too slow, for the club came down and half stunned him, and when he fully recovered his senses he found himself within stone walls. At the examination, Jonathan Wild swore against him, and his partner in the burglary supported the thief-taker, so Sheppard was committed for further examination and sent to the New Prison at Clerkenwell. That was on the 24th of May, 1724, and on the day following, the jailer entered the cell to find a broken file on the floor and the window bars forced, but of the prisoner there was no sign. How the young thief had reached the ground and climbed the wall of the prison yard was never known.

For a time Jack Sheppard seemed to have vanished, and some reported him dead, but any lingering doubts that Jonathan Wild might have had, relative to the young man's existence, were dispelled when he heard rumors of a plan to make a glorious haul by burglarizing no less a place than the cellars beneath his own private residence. A little cunning questioning, a little shrewd investigating and Mr. Wild had his plans laid. So, one day, when Jack repaired to the Blue Boar where he was to meet his new associates, he encountered Wild, who looked at him like a ponderous wildcat. For a moment they regarded one another with appreciative eyes.

"If you was dead," said Jack with an oath, "I'd get somewhere. It's always you stops me."

"If I wasn't Wild, I'd like to be Jack Sheppard,"

said the thief-taker with a sort of sneering laugh, and foolish Jack was pleased with the left-handed compliment, drawing himself up and expanding his chest. Wild added, "But this time you go to Newgate, young man. From there you will not escape."

"Try me and see," said Jack boastfully.

No more was said then, and, at a sign, officers appeared and Jack was marched off to Newgate. Six days later, on Monday, August 31st, 1724, the death warrant was received and the prison-breaker was placed on exhibition in the condemned hold, visitors paying a guinea a head to look at him.

Then for the rascal there was the Stone Jug, the strong room that had held Claude Duval, a room from which none had escaped.

"You'll not get out of this place," said the jailer.

"But it is my business to escape," retorted the boastful Jack.

"And mine to see that you do not escape!" was the reply.

"Then let each attend well to his business," crowed Jack.

It would seem that Jack attended to his with more assiduity than the jailer. At any rate his thoughts were always on escape, the thoughts of the jailer only partially on detention. But under the eye of the head turnkey the young thief was heavily chained, doors, window bars and locks well examined, chains tested and padlock handled, then, satisfied that at last the prison-breaker was effectively checkmated, the door was slammed and the bolt turned. The jailers betook themselves to the ward room where was a good fire, for the night was chilly, and before long, to make assurance doubly sure, to the end that the head turnkey might sleep in peace, a jailer was despatched to make sure that all was well. Grumblingly, the fellow went, complaining against those who could not believe their own senses.

—2—

The whole thing was far too real for dreaming and the jailer shut his eyes and opened them again. Less than an hour before, he had left Jack Sheppard fast chained to an iron bar that ran the length of the cell, a stone cell lighted by one small iron-barred window set nine feet from the floor; and now of the prisoner there was no sign. He satisfied himself of the fastening of the door, stood for half a minute pondering, then left the place to call his superior, taking care to see to it that the door was tight. In three minutes he returned, talking volubly to his chief as he flung open the door suddenly, that the head turnkey might get something of the shock that he had experienced, and was astounded to see the youthful prisoner seated on the floor, chained as he should have been. So all that the jailer got for his pains was a sound berating, in answer to which he had nothing to say and tried to cover his confusion with some half-hearted facetiousness.

HIGHWAYMEN

What had happened was this: No sooner had the door slammed upon Sheppard when he was first thrust in there, than he set to work with a piece of stiff wire which he had concealed in his clothes, and, before long, succeeded in picking the padlock. That left him free from the floor bar, though the gyves were still about his ankles and the heavy fetters were joined by a long chain. Once free to move about, he picked up the clattering chain, muffled it with his stockings and went to the chimney to explore. No fire had been in the fireplace for years, so his venture was the easier for that. Climbing, he found the chimney passage barred with an iron rod worked into the walls at about eight feet from the hearthstone. It was while examining the iron fastenings that he heard the clatter of the feet of the returning jailer, so he remained quiet until there came to him the sharp exclamation of surprise and the noise of the slamming door, when he descended swiftly, refastened the padlock and took a position as if he had not moved since first he was thrust in that place.

The head turnkey, though he laughed at the jailer's tale, was well aware that Sheppard was a slippery fellow, and, in the interests of security, gave orders that he should be handcuffed in addition to being fettered and fastened to the floor rod. There was another reason for the extra precaution. Visitors of note were expected that day. For the popular admiration of the notorious criminal had filled high and low and spread far, even to royalty itself. The dramatic interest of it all so touched the king that he commanded Sir James Thornhill to go to Newgate and paint the criminal's picture, and the turnkey had been notified accordingly. Hence the extra chains.

Others had been interested in the young criminal. On 'Change Alley, Sir Richard Steele had chanced to meet the poet, John Gay, and they had repaired to a coffee house where they sat long, talking of crime and criminals in general, and of the highwaymen Blueskin and Jack Sheppard in particular, and Gay had invited Steele to go with him to Newgate. That invitation was declined, Steele saying that in the army he had met rascals enough. So Gay decided to go alone.

Nor would Hogarth, who loved to picture the beast in man, be one to lose so glorious an opportunity. Chancing to pass a gymnasium in Oxford Street, the painter of vice in its ugliness was halted when he saw the notable, James Figg, teacher of boxing and broadsword, who had broken the jaw of a young giant from Venice who called himself the Venetian Gondolier, and then had challenged all England. Hogarth sketched Figg and, meanwhile, the pugilist told him of his intention to visit Newgate and see the young fellow who would soon be hanged. So it came to pass that on October 15th, 1724, the brilliantly dressed John Gay with eyes bright and shining, in arm with Sir James Thornhill, had entered into the gates of England's strongest prison. Not more than ten minutes had they been there when Hogarth and the prize-fighter were admitted.

It was quite characteristic of Jack Sheppard, as of nearly all criminals, that vanity in him was easily awakened. In his own world of thieves and sharpers and rascals he was already a hero, and the fact that his picture was to be painted for the king, flattered him immensely. Then, too, his visitors played upon his self-esteem. The good-natured Gay said many things which the prisoner treasured in his heart, especially when he quoted Pope, saying: "Let but fortune favor us, and the world will sure admire." That nerved Jack somehow. But especially did the talk interest Jack when the good-natured, gusty Defoe dropped in as the visit was about to end, for he learned then that Defoe had not only stood in the pillory, but had also sat in Newgate prison, and to the highwayman, a prisoner was necessarily a criminal. Then Gay and the journalist with very honest eyes, vied with each other spiritedly in the exaltation of daring men of the past who had flouted authority—Robin Hood, Captain Kidd, Colonel Blood.

"And perhaps," said Defoe, "his Majesty may be induced to grant a pension to our Jack as the King did to the man who stole his crown. Certainly, I went from a King's chamber to Newgate, so why should not Jack Sheppard go from Newgate to a King's chamber? Egad! I'd like well enough to see him at Guildhall on Lord Mayor's Day."

That both journalist and poet were but playing a game of conversational beggar-my-neighbor never entered the prisoner's head. He sat open-mouthed, only half understanding the meaning of much that was said, seeing himself something very much like a martyred hero, an immortal. The suggestions of Guildhall pleased him vastly, and Gay's quotation, "Let but fortune favor us and the world will sure admire," rang in his ears. To him, admiration was the breath of life.

—3—

The visitors left at noon, and at one the jailer brought the food that was to last the prisoner for the rest of the day. As soon as the man had gone, Jack Sheppard set to work. He had, he well knew, at least eight hours before his cell would be visited again, except for accidents, for the night watch would not go the rounds until the bell of St. Sepulchre's Church struck ten. As for the corridor guards, they were not apt to be marching up and down a cold stone corridor on a chilly night when below was a roaring fire and tobacco and drink and good company of its kind.

It was no easy task to free his hands, but, unhardened by toil, they were slender, and, by dint of the use of some of the paint oil that Sir James Thornhill had left, he managed to draw them out of the handcuffs though the operation was somewhat painful. The padlock, picked before, offered no serious problem, but he could not divest himself of the chains joining the ankle rings. So he contrived to fasten the middle link to his belt, drew the fetters up high on his calves, and, thus hampered, applied himself to the task which lay before him.

No time was lost in chimney exploration. He had laid plans while his portrait was being painted and had enormous confidence in himself. With his piece of wire he commenced to scratch away the mortar above the fireplace and at last extracted a brick, thus gaining the first important step to freedom. To make the hole larger was easy. Brick followed brick until a pile of rubbish had accumulated upon the stone floor and the hole above the mantel was large enough to permit squeezing through. Standing on the mantel and reaching in, he dislodged bricks until he had released the iron bar that blocked the chimney way. That was killing two birds with one stone, not only giving him a way of escape, but also furnishing him with a kind of rough crowbar of square iron an inch in thickness and three feet long, an invaluable tool for prison-breaking.

Having compared notes with fellow criminals, he had some general knowledge of the plan of the building. So, with great daring, he resolved to break through, by way of the chimney, into the cell above the chamber from which he had escaped, a place known as the Red Room, used for state prisoners only, and, to his certain knowledge, then vacant. He half expected to find an open door in the tenantless cell. In the chimney, his knees braced against one wall and his back against the other, and using his iron bar as a pick, he succeeded in opening a hole into the Red Room in far shorter time than that in which he had broken out of his own cell.

Crawling through, he found, to his disappointment, that he had entered a place in every respect similar to that which he had left, and he was full of a kind of perplexed resentment. There was the same kind of barred window the same height from the floor, there was a door barred in exactly the same way as that below, and there was the unreachable ceiling. Obviously, the way of escape was to be through the door. Some time was spent in an attempt to pick the lock with his iron wire, but soon he gave up the effort. There seemed to be a better, an easier way if he dared to take the chance of being noisy. The lock was heavy and square, more than a foot each way, and the plate of it was studded with heavy-headed nails. With his bar, Jack Sheppard tried hammering at one of the nail heads, striking sideways, and succeeded in battering off the head of it. Twelve nails in all he thus broke and was rewarded by seeing the lock plate fall off. To draw the bolt was then easy.

He found himself in a dark and a narrow passage, a kind of stone sloping gallery which led to the prison chapel, but it was pitchy dark there. Feeling his way, he came to another door securely locked and large enough to fill the space from wall to wall. Unluckily for him, the door offered a smooth surface, the lock being on the farther side. For a moment he grappled with the problem, attacking the wall with his bar at a point where he judged the bolt would shoot into the boxing; he started to powder the stone, making a free passage for the still extended bolt, and, after some severe labor, threw open the door.

For the first time since he had left his cell he was in a well-lighted place. It was the chapel, and he found himself in the roofless cage in which those condemned to death sat to hear services. Up the cage he clambered, getting over the spiked top clumsily, being hampered with his chains. While passing over, a link in his chain entangled with a spike and he came near to falling headlong, but a quick jerk broke the spike off at the neck. His new environment was a kind of passage-way, with a grilled partition separating it from the portion of the chapel used by less desperate prisoners. The iron grilling extended to the ceiling and the way out was through a locked gate. The lock, however, was lighter than any he had yet encountered and he shattered it with a couple of blows with his bar. He stepped into that part of the chapel from which there were two exits, one by a door leading to the prison roof, the other by a door leading to the debtor's prison; both doors were locked.

The way to the roof was the route chosen and he forced the lock by hammering off the heavy studs which held the lock plate, as he had done in the case of the Red Room door. There was a disappointment for him in that the door gave, not directly upon the roof as he had supposed, but into a short passage at the end of which was another door: the fifth he had encountered. Feeling that, except for ill chance, he was far from human ears, for the chapel was only used on Sundays and special occasions, he attacked the new obstacle boldly with his bar. The job proved to be far tougher than he had anticipated, for he could not get at the nail-heads by reason of their being rounded. Going back to the chapel, he found the spike that had been broken off, and, taking it with him, again went to the door. The spike he used as a wedge, hammering it with his bar between oaken plank and iron lock, and thus prizing off the boxing.

One imagines him flushed, dusty, thirsting and breathless, his task seemingly done, his hopes high, with the saying of Gay's that so captivated him, ringing in his ears. Given a kind fortune, and there was an admiring world waiting. So he flung open the door, hopeful of seeing the sky at last, only to find himself in another gloomy passage and, at the end, a door with a formidable lock. "A lock," says an old writer, "more than a foot wide, strongly plated and girded to the door with thick iron hoops. Below it a prodigiously large iron bolt was shot into the socket and, in order to keep it there, was fastened with a hasp and further protected with an immense padlock. Besides this, the door was crossed and recrossed by iron bars, clenched by broadheaded nails. An iron fillet secured the socket of the bolt and the box of the lock to the main post of the doorway."

Jack Sheppard stood a long time examining that. For a man well equipped with tools it would have been a serious business to undertake the forcing of such a door, but for a fellow armed only with a clumsy iron bar, hampered with a heavy chain hanging to him, his legs galled with rough iron fetters, working in semi-obscurity and wearied with what he had done already, it was a serious problem. An hour he wrought without making any progress, making matters worse indeed by breaking the tip of his spike and bending his bar. Once he became panic-stricken, fancying that the wardens had discovered his escape and were hot on his trail. And how the time was flying he did not know, could only dimly guess indeed. Soon his physical fatigue asserted itself and he was bound to rest awhile.

Attempting his task again he succeeded at last in forcing off the great iron bar that ran up along the door post, a piece of metal all of seven feet long, seven inches wide and two inches thick. Sheppard regarded his work with a kind of awed satisfaction, then threw open the door. Outside was a short flight of steps at the head of which stood a door that opened outwards, but the key was in the lock. Here at last was kind fortune on his side. A moment later he found himself on the prison roof, and, as he stepped forth, the bell of

St. Sepulchre's Church rang out, and he counted eight strokes. Six hours had passed since he left his cell.

Jack Sheppard had no time to abandon himself to agreeable musings, although he had gained the open. He was, it is true, on the flat roof of the prison, but the roof was all of forty feet from the street, and, moreover, it was enclosed by a wall that ran straight up, without projection or crevice, for fourteen feet. It was discouraging, but resolutely he ignored the idea of giving up the task he had undertaken. The nearer to freedom, the stronger his determination. The very street sounds that came to his ears nerved him, filled him with hope and encouragement. In his perplexity, the idea of using the door he had last passed through, came as a flash. All of eight feet high it was, and, standing upon it he found it easy to reach the coping of the wall. He drew himself up, though the chain hampered him terribly.

Astride of the wall he reviewed his situation. On his left was another roof, the roof of the chapel, but clearly nothing was to be gained by dropping on to that. So he worked his way, inch by inch, a leg on either side of the wall, his dragging chain catching frequently, until he arrived at the outer corner. There was a moment of triumph for him, but swift came a fear. His triumph was the sight of the street, the yellow lamp lights and lanterns and flaring torches, the people, the coaches, the sedan chairs; and his mind became full of the notion of notoriety that would be his when his escape was discovered. But the fear came at the sight of the precipice of brick, a sheer fall of more than fifty feet.

The booming of the church bell as it tolled the half hour, startled him from his dreaming. He was losing altogether too much time, and, did his keepers discover his escape, recapture was inevitable. Along the coping of the wall he worked his way until he turned the other corner and there was a new hope. Twenty feet below was the blackened roof of a house, and, though the roof was sharply pointed and tiled, the coping of the wall touched the prison wall. Yet even twenty feet was far too great a distance to drop in the dark, shackled as he was. Had he been without chains on his legs he would not have so hesitated; but a chain might mean a broken leg or ankle. So back he worked his way—back along the wall that hung over the street, back to the open door, down to the roof, into the passage and past door after door, through the chapel and over the spiked barrier, along the passage into the Red Room, back into the chimney and down to his own cell again, where the sight of the floor piled with bricks and mortar almost startled him.

Now he was very nervous, for he seemed to hear the shooting of bolts and the muffled slamming of doors, and, certainly, the time of the coming of the night watch might not be so far away. For a moment he hesitated, half deciding to wait and make an attempt on the jailer, but, weighing the chances and knowing that the path ahead was clear, he abandoned the idea. In another moment he had taken the bed coverings and was stripping them, improvising a rough rope. To the chimney again, into the state chamber and onward he went. There was little time to lose now. Nor did he forget to carry his spike along. On that much was to hang.

Strange and interesting ideas filled his mind as, seated astride the wall again, he worked with his spike to fashion a hole in which he might set the iron point as a peg. From the talk of Gay and Defoe, he had learned of the handsome way in which the King had treated the man Blood who had stolen the crown jewels. Why should he not be equally well treated? Had the present king not been interested enough to have Jack Sheppard's portrait painted? Had not a writer and a poet been to see him? Greater than all, to his thinking, had not the most famous prize-fighter in all England shaken him by the hand and called him a bold fellow? Surely, then, the street once gained, those who walked there, now all unconscious of his daring, would not hesitate to acclaim him as a hero. He felt as an exiled king must do when he learns of a nation waiting with welcoming arms.

At last the spike was fixed, a little insecurely to be sure, but still hopefully lodged. To it he hung the end of his blanket rope, and, laying his body across the coping, put his weight on the line gradually. It held well, and he reached the house roof in safety.

HIGHWAYMEN

Through a hatchway half-way up the roof he made his way and into a cluttered attic, then down a short flight of stairs and through a door, to find himself in a bedroom where slept a man and his wife. A creaking board on which Sheppard stepped awakened the man and he called out, at which the prisoner had the utmost difficulty to prevent himself from making a dash and resting his chances upon his strength and his speed. But the sleeper sought his pillow again and Sheppard took another step. This time his irons clanked and the man fully awoke.

"Hello!" he cried, and sat up again.

Sheppard made no move.

"Who's there?" challenged the householder. Fancying that some one was at the door he left his bed and peered into the passage, but seeing no one, returned to bed. That act, for Sheppard, was a salvation. Knowing the exit, his task was a hundredfold easier. With a sudden dash he was at the door and had it open, passed through, slammed it behind him and, half a minute later was in the street. Out of the window the householder's head was thrust and his voice was heard bellowing, "Watch! Watch! A thief! A thief!" Other windows were flung open and screaming voices took up the cry.

At that, people in the street came running: men from nearby houses with sticks and staves and pokers, some in slippers and nightcaps; a watchman or two with lantern and staff; boys and dogs and a clattering horseman; fellows from the tavern; a little group of fashionable fellows with drawn swords intent on a night of mischief as Mohocks and glad of any excitement that offered. The very thickness of the crowd with people swarming in one another's way was an aid to Sheppard. He added his cries of "Thief!" to the din, slipped down a dark alley and none noticed him.

Near midnight he found himself in a small street near Shoe Lane and there he broke into the house of a locksmith and sat in the dark, filing at his irons, no heroic figure indeed, but a kind of immature young man with short-cropped hair, rather narrow shoulders, a snub nose and a weak chin. Freed from his fetters, he broke into a haberdashery house, then into a draper's in Fleet Street, where he made his entry by way of the cellar grating. In each place he robbed the till, and, presently stepped into the street dressed in a fine claret-colored coat, knee breeches and buckled shoes. At last he was Jack Sheppard free, but also Jack Sheppard purposeless, without a plan, vaguely hunting the notoriety that he considered his due.

So a first day went past, a day spent, for the most part, in wandering from tavern to tavern, sometimes meeting, sometimes avoiding, old acquaintances, and, towards evening, standing in the streets listening, with a keen sense of enjoyment, to the ballad monger's singing and offering for sale The True Story of Jack Sheppard's Escape from Newgate. Their nasal whining was as golden music to him as they chanted:

"Jack Sheppard came from Willesden,
From Willesden town came he,
As bold a lad and daring,
As ever ye did see.

'O, stand sir and deliver!'
He cried, this lad so bold,
To him there was surrendered,
A purse all fat with gold."

There was much more of it and his deeds of violence and lawlessness were intermingled with those of other nefarious rascals, but to Sheppard it was the fame he craved. Telesicrates of Cyrene, when he had won the foot race in armor, could have felt no more proud than did Sheppard when he heard the comments of the bystanders on his own exploits. The world that he knew talked of him, and he was well content. For him, the ballad singer was a brilliant lyric artist, a gifted and courtly eulogist. Naturally, he soon gravitated to his old quarters, met his former cronies and plates clattered and glasses clinked.

—4—

The Lord Mayor of London had no idea of entertaining, or being entertained by a criminal on the occasion of his Guildhall Feast, but Master Sheppard, brave with drink and full of an idea of his own importance, deemed the occasion one not to be missed. While the trumpets sounded a fanfare in the street and the procession passed Temple Bar—the cavalcade with its golden coach and eight horses, its armored knights, its minstrels and beadles on horseback, its fluttering silken banners and proud city companies gorgeously costumed—the man who had escaped from Newgate prison drifted doubtfully on the edge of things. Finding Guildhall, he had been awed by four halberdiers at the outer gate, so he sought the rear entrance, found the great kitchen, entered undetected and watched things with startled eyes. That such magnificence was in the world astonished him beyond measure. The great fireplace, sixteen feet long and seven feet high, the roaring coal fire before which slowly turned a gigantic piece of beef all of five hundred pounds in weight, the half hundred cooks and helpers, the crowd of servers and dish-carriers coming and going and every one gay and bright-eyed, the astonishing display of soup tureens and plates and dishes; the sight took his breath. It all impressed the simple fellow as extraordinarily vast and complicated.

His dream had been to enter into some small hall, to proclaim his name and forthwith to be hailed as hero. Instead, the time had come, and he felt himself to be a misfit, a something very small and insignificant. At the back of his head he meditated, but he was still vainglorious with drink. His mind passed to his companions and the promise made to them that he would declare himself. But what then had seemed easy, now assumed vast proportions. The very atmosphere here was all new to him, the atmosphere of cleanliness, of

HIGHWAYMEN 71

activity, of order. Then he became aware of a short, fat, important kind of man with a plump, pink face who stood regarding him with an unfriendly eye, the corner of his apron in his hand. The fat man wanted to know Sheppard's business, what he did there, how he had gained an entrance.

Mr. Sheppard moistened his dry lips with his tongue and essayed some explanation. It struck him that things were far from turning out as he had expected, but he murmured something. What he said was inaudible to the fat man, who showed signs of anger. A disagreeable doubt began to possess Jack and his eye lighted upon the exit as he heard the fat man growl another question. Again Sheppard spoke, this time saying something about his fearing no man and no prison built for man, but his speech was blurred and clipped, and he was silenced by the aproned man, who took him by the collar with a firm grip and started to hustle him to the door. It might have been well for Sheppard had he kept his fame to himself, but a suggestion born of Defoe's remark came to his muddled mind. He had visions, too, of Colonel Blood, the highwayman who became a crown pensioner somehow. So Jack Sheppard wriggled and strove to release himself from the fat man's grasp. Under the influence of the heat and the excitement, his voice had become thicker, his legs unsteadier. Things seemed about to collapse.

"Loose me! Loose me, man!" he cried. "I am Jack Sheppard." Then, that there might be no misconception, he added, "Jack Sheppard who broke out of Newgate prison."

His declaration was quite lost upon his captor.

"I'll Jack Sheppard you, young fellow," said the fat man, touched with a certain warmth of indignation. "A drunken rascal you are, and one with a graceless face." So saying, he hustled the wriggling lad to the door. "Out to the kennel with you, and take yourself off before I call the watch."

One or two by the fire laughed at the struggle, thinking the drunken man but a common interloper, for, the kitchen door being unguarded, two or three curious citizens had found their way there that day. But a merry youth whose hands were white with flour came in from a passage-way at the moment when Jack Sheppard called his name, and, a moment later, had joined in the fray. Down he ducked and his strong arms gripped Sheppard's kicking legs.

"I tell you I'm Jack Sheppard and I want to see the Lord Mayor," said the wine-bold fellow.

"He is indeed Jack Sheppard," said the flour-white lad in no way relaxing his grip. "Moreover, there is a reward for his capture, so hold him fast until the watch comes."

At that the importance of his capture dawned on the fat cook and he fell into a state of vast activity. Off came his apron and in another moment it was about Sheppard's head, and the man from Newgate was bellowing and blustering. Another came to his aid and onlookers offered suggestions.

"Into the coal cellar with him," said the baker's lad, and, emboldened by the manifest weakness of the enemy, he lifted him bodily, thrust him in the cellar and securely bolted the door. And there Jack Sheppard was left to meditate upon the fickleness of fortune, until the watch came and he was again on his way to Newgate.

—5—

A week later, on November 16th, 1724, the prison-breaker made his last appearance in public. The ordinary flow of people going to and fro was checked, and sightseers stood before Newgate in the chill and drizzle to watch the condemned man on his way to the gallows. In a two-wheeled cart, seated upon his coffin, was the prisoner, and with him was a minister of the church. Before and behind rode guards, and a file of soldiers brought up the rear. At the Crown Inn there was a brief halt, where, according to custom, the landlord presented the prisoner with a bowl of drink, and Jack Sheppard made his last flourish, standing in the cart and toasting the crowd, while some, of sentimental bent, pressed near to shake him by the hand.

Then the procession moved on towards Tyburn and the ragtag and bobtail of the town followed, some in wagons, the most of them on foot; roughs and toughs, loafers and criminals were there; children ran at the heels of bedraggled women and sometimes entire families were crowded in shop carts on the way to see the sight. There were lowering and savage men and unkempt youths from the riverside, and hawkers drove a good trade selling cakes and baubles. For an execution was a public festival in those days, and a sight in which well-dressed men and foul-mouthed fellows in rags alike were interested. So the cart rattled over the rough ways, down Oxford Street, past Edgeware Road, the crowd in the rear of it increasing, a fighting, blundering, tumultuous mob; a mass of half-savage human beings pressing on one another—and the goal was the black and ugly Thing around which a crowd already jostled. Indeed, the men at arms had much ado to clear a path for the cart and, afterwards, to keep the crowd back while the hangman was busy with grim technicalities.

No sooner had the sentence been executed than the vigilance of the men-at-arms was relaxed. Then, from the crowd a big-bodied man pushed and he was followed by half-a-dozen others, some with sticks, some with butchers' tools, some with heavy bludgeons. The swarthy-faced fellow faced the crowd and his black hair fell over his eyes.

"Blueskin to the rescue!" some one shouted and the cry was taken up on all sides. "Blueskin! Blueskin!"

It was the partner and companion of Jack Sheppard. Some have said that the dash of Blueskin was a spectacular affair arranged by Defoe, and the newspapers of that day contained a paragraph leading to the supposition that Defoe was to obtain from the condemned man, at the last moment, a signed confession. On the cart Blueskin stood a moment doubtfully, then he severed the rope, and the body of the prison-breaker fell to earth. At the same moment there came a volley of firing from the soldiers, and Blueskin the highwayman stood a moment, swaying heavily, then toppled over the side of the cart, shot through the chest. A few of Sheppard's cronies seized his body and carried it away to Willesden, where it was buried, but what became of the body of Blueskin, no one seems to know and fewer to care. At any rate, a tale of shame was ended and there was one rogue the less in the world.

DICK TURPIN

" . . . Sam Weller burst at once into the following wild and beautiful legend: . . .

ROMANCE

Bold Turpin vunce on Hounslow Heath,
His bold mare Bess bestrode-er:
Ven there he seed the Bishop's coach
A-comin' along the road-er.
So he galloped close to the horses' legs
And he claps his head vithin:
And the Bishop says, "Sure as eggs is eggs
This here's the bold Turpin!"

CHORUS

And the Bishop says, "Sure as eggs is eggs,
This here's the bold Turpin!"

Says Turpin, "You shall eat your words,
With a sarse of leaden bul-let,"
So he puts a pistol to his mouth,
And he fires it down his gul-let,
The coachman he not likin' the job,
Set off at a full gallop
But Dick put a couple of balls in his nob
And perwailed on him to stop.

CHORUS (sarcastically)

But Dick put a couple of balls in his nob
And perwailed on him to stop.

—*Pickwick Papers.*

DICK TURPIN

DICK TURPIN was a highwayman and many a man and many a coach did he stop on the road, and his name was known at widely separated places, at Harrogate as well as Epping, at Bath and at Epsom quite as well as at Tunbridge Wells. Indeed, he never failed to announce his name to those he robbed, and many counted it as a noteworthy thing to have been stopped by him. Tales were told of how, dressed in the height of fashion, he had rented great wainscoted rooms in Soho and entertained, not the gentry to be sure, but tough spirits of his own kidney. And once, according to tradition, he surprised Mr. Pope of Twickenham as he walked in the fields, but found nothing on the man except a bundle of papers which the poet seemed to be trying to hide, so after looking through them, the highwayman tossed the bundle into a hedge. Seeing the little man run to his papers, Turpin, full of suspicion, took them again suspecting some hidden treasure that he had possibly overlooked, but there was nothing but scrawling writing. So the thief counted it gain when he returned the papers and was handed a gold chain which had been overlooked, knowing nothing of the treasure that lay hidden in the Essay on Man. For all that the highwayman was twitted shortly afterwards by the witty and charming Mrs. Bellenden when he stopped her coach on Hownslow Heath. When he called on her to deliver her jewels to him she flung her rings into his face, calling him a dull boor who did not know real treasure from silly gold, she having in mind the Twickenham affair. But what she meant, he did not at all understand.

In the year 1739, Dick Turpin, the Thaxted butcher's son, whose real name was Tom Palmer, had an encounter that yielded nothing but disappointment, though there hung on it an adventure the tale of which all England loves to this day. The Briton does not readily relinquish his heroes of popular mythology, and romance hangs to the tale of Turpin, true or false, as it hangs to the tale of King Alfred and the cakes, or the tale of Guy Fawkes and his gunpowder barrel, or to the tale of Sweeny Todd, the Demon Barber of number 186 Fleet Street, who is said to have robbed unwary customers and converted them into meat pies. So here is the tale of Turpin, and on part of it at least, the finger of certitude may be placed.

One day, Turpin, a fellow splendid enough with his silver-mounted horse trappings and pistols and sword:

his coat of scarlet and his satin waistcoat: and last, but most important, his bonny mare Black Bess, rode down from Chingford way. He saw, and noted a drover taking cattle Londonward. Now, his knowledge of his former trade told him that animals in such condition would bring a good, round price, whereupon he laid his plans carefully and renewed a somewhat sagging acquaintance with the ostler at the Cow and Tub Inn. After a while, he learned from the ostler that, on a certain Wednesday, the cattle man would leave London bound for his home in Fyfield.

The way to the village of Fyfield led through Epping Forest, and, having checked up the ostler's information by private observation, not only seeing the drover prepare for the journey at the Inn, but also watching him as he passed through Hackney, Turpin loosed his rein and cantered easily to the River Ching, a little willow-bordered stream, and there waited in patience to the end that he might levy tribute on the returning farmer. But the cattle man was far longer in getting to that place than the highwayman's calculations had led him to expect; indeed, the western sky was red and gold before he appeared. At length he came in sight, a broad-faced, jolly-looking, corpulent fellow on a slow nag, riding unsuspiciously across the patch of heathy open land which Dick commanded from his hiding-place. Seeing that all was ripe for action, the highwayman leaped to saddle and went into the road with a dash, drawing rein sharply so that Black Bess blocked the road and halted the red-faced drover. Then out came Dick's sword with a flourish and the point of it was at the farmer's chest.

"Stand and deliver!" cried Turpin.

The farmer's horse stopped mechanically, and, the reins being loosed, it fell to cropping the herbage between the cart ruts as if being halted on the king's highway was an ordinary occurrence and an everyday matter. As for the man, he turned his large blue eyes on the dashing highway robber, and, in the patient tone of one who is resigned to all things, said:

"Standing I already am, but I have nothing to deliver."

"None of your nonsense," exclaimed Turpin, a little staggered with the bull-necked affirmation. "In London you sold cattle and sold them well. Where is the money?"

The red-faced man gave a little laugh, then said: "Would that I knew. True I sold well, but—"

"No excuses," interrupted Turpin impatiently. "Out with your purse and quickly."

He was brisk, and acted in a competent and business-like manner, making a little thrust with his blade in the air, but the drover remained unexcited.

"I have no love for your weapon," observed the farmer with vast gravity. "Why not put it aside, lad? The truth is that my purse, and all that was in it was taken by one of your trade less than an hour ago, and on this side of Buckhurst Hill, and mighty vexed the fellow seemed to be at the sorry showing I made. Only a couple of shillings had I, though he searched me well, believing I lied when I said that I had no more."

"What!" roared Dick. "Two shillings?"

The man nodded his head by way of reply and there was something in his solid calmness which led the highwayman to believe that he spoke the truth. "If you lie—" he blustered, then dropped the point of his sword.

The farmer who had been turning things over in his mind, laughed a little softly. "So also said the other fellow who stopped me," he said. "He made me take off my boots and he went through my pockets, but nothing did he find. Two shillings I had when I left London, with which I intended to pay my fare to-night at Epping Inn, but now that, too, is gone. Luckily they know me there for an honest man, and money or no money, I may stay there for the night. To be sure, the fellow at Buckhurst Hill wished me well at parting, but little good are his wishes when he leaves me penniless."

The straightforward heartiness of the man woke a kind of delight in human fellowship in Dick Turpin, so he returned his sword to its scabbard, saying that he would ride a little way with him for company's sake.

"But what of the money that you had for the cattle you sold?" he asked, and the farmer laughed softly as he tugged at his rein to lift his nag's head, and, seeing that there was no more to fear from the highwayman, thumped the ribs of his animal with his heels.

"Little of the money that a man earns does he keep," grumbled the farmer. "To be sure, I sold my cattle at a good price, as you say, but many were the hands stretched out to take it before I could put it in my purse. Like hawks after young chicks are men after money in the city. There was the man who owns the land that I till, and to his agent went nine-tenths of what I had. There was a lawyer, too, with papers, and him I had to fee. Much more there was."

A silence fell then as they rode together, and when the farmer again spoke there was a good-humored smile on his face and he looked at Turpin out of the tail of his eyes. "If all the men that you stop on the road are in like sorry case, then is your business as bad as mine, I think."

The highwayman made no reply, but merely rubbed his ear with vexation, so the farmer went on in his dull, monotonous way, with many windings and loopings, to tell of this and of that and of the other. So it came about that Turpin heard much of London, and of how his companion had visited Hallam's Booth where he had seen and heard the affecting tragedy of The Trial and Ancient History of Fair Rosamund, "the which," he said, "I am sure would wring tears from a heart of stone. For seeing the sweet wench so sad, I had a mind to run to her side." Then there was a long tale of how he had gone with a lawyer's clerk to Marylebone Gardens and there heard martial music, and also saw a Punch and Judy show at which he "laughed until the tears ran," though while he watched, some light-fingered fellow had taken his watch.

So they rode and talked until the moon came up, when, becoming aware of a clatter of horse hoofs in the distance, Dick bade his farmer farewell and turned his mare's head to plunge into the nearest cover, which chanced to be a grove of tall oaks.

Turpin discarded all concealment a few minutes later when he saw that the coming rider was alone and riding fast. When the horseman was a dozen yards away, he guided Black Bess into the middle of the road and turned, as though going in the same direction as the coming rider. The horseman coming alongside, he drew his pistol, leaned over and caught at the other's bridle, shouting as he did so, "Stand! Your money or your life!"

"Neither!" roared the other as he pushed his steed in such way as to shoulder Black Bess, and, at a glance, Dick Turpin recognized his friend and fellow highwayman, Tom King.

"Business must be bad indeed," said King, "when you stop a man who has but two shillings which he took from a farmer," and at that Dick stared at him dolefully.

"Bad indeed," he made reply. "Five men and a coach have I stopped since Monday, and not enough to pay an ostler. It seems to me that there is no more money in the world."

The pair stood with nothing to say, then dismounted

and sat under a tree, while the horses, with reins hanging loose, softly munched the grass. Falling to talk presently there were comparisons and the relating of experiences, with much bewailing because of the sad days on which they had fallen. Presently Tom King advanced a theory that where men were few, as in the country, money must perforce be scanty. Wealth, he said, was to be had only by bold doings in the towns where were roaring crowds and bustling multitudes. Then, like the farmer, Tom King told tales of what he had seen, of gay throngs at Vauxhall Gardens where men and women played for high stakes, of taverns merry with the sound of French horns, and of many glimmering lights in pleasure gardens where people sat at tables eating and drinking and singing until the early hours of the morning.

In a limited way Dick Turpin had imagination, and, while his knowledge of London was confined to the smaller streets and alleys in the neighborhood of Drury Lane for the most part, yet, when he heard the tales told by Tom King, he began to picture himself moving in a fashionable throng, passing as an honest citizen, and, by some deed of derring-do, winning a fortune at a single swoop. His idea of what might actually be done was hazy in the extreme, but there was the certainty that he had fallen on evil days and so anything promised more than his present way of life.

HIGHWAYMEN

—2—

A few days later, Tom King and Dick Turpin sat in the bow window of an ale-house overlooking the river Thames, idly watching the boats as they discharged crowds of brilliantly-dressed men and women bound for Vauxhall Gardens. For Turpin it was a wonderful sight to see a great barge, adorned with flags and streamers, its band of music and chattering and laughing pleasure-lovers.

Seated near them was a rustily-dressed fellow of nervous ways who drank glass after glass of wine, and on whom Turpin looked with a kind of awe. The man seemed to know the names and conditions of every great personage, and made a running commentary upon the figures as they passed. "That," said he, "is Walpole, who dropped five thousand the other night at cards, and with him is Lord Chesterfield. No. Not the big man with the red face: that's Fielding. The other, I mean, with the beetled brow. Walpole rode two horses to death hastening to tell the King that his father was dead. The drunken man behind him, he with the lady, is Lord Granby. A merry rascal that. He has doubtless come from Jenny Whim's tavern in Chelsea." There was much more of it, and Turpin was all ear. Particularly was he eager to know more of Walpole the rider.

"I have a mare," he said, "that I will ride against

your Walpole." But the rusty man laughed at that. "I knew him at Eton," said the rustily-dressed man. "A Norfolk family and proud, every one of them with an eye for a horse and a hand for a playing card."

At the garden gate Dick stared in heavy wonder at the line of coaches and the silken ladies who descended from them, and, once in the garden, his delight was unbounded. The sound of the great organ playing something that set the people to clapping their hands, the great paintings here and there, the strange mechanical toys with painted landscapes and little coaches that moved along miniature roads, the tiny river with toy boats and splashing cascade and water mill, the figures of wood which walked and sat and disappeared into caves; all these things charmed the simple highwayman to the point of loud admiration, and it amazed him that amidst all, young gallants walked, taking no more heed of the things about them than he would take of the furze bushes on Hampstead Heath. Then, too, there were the parading masks, the wine parties, the wax-lighted summer houses and the glitter and the sparkle and the fine dresses. Dick Turpin was like a child in a great toy shop, and well-nigh distracted with it all.

So the two knights of the road, who were dressed as bravely as any there, wandered up and down the winding paths, taking no hand in the festivities, with Tom King, more sophisticated than his friend, keeping a sharp lookout for possible business. After much walking they came, quite unexpectedly, upon a quiet corner where was a summer house of latticed work all grown about with climbing plants. Within, a little party of four sat at cards around a table lit with a dozen wax candles set in glass bowls. There, too, sat the tall man with deep-set eyes and a Roman nose, whom their rusty friend of the riverside inn had named as Henry Fielding; but he was watching the players, apparently a friend. In contrast with the players with their gold bedizened clothes, he was plainly dressed in a snuff-colored brown suit, but his occasional bursts of loud, boisterous laughter made him seem the gayest one there.

The sight of so much gold coin, heaped on the table, arrested the attention of the highwaymen, and Tom King checked his companion and drew him aside to the cover of a laurel bush in the rear of the summer house. Then there were whispered plans, tentative plans, impossible plans. Could one dash in and destroy the lights while the other seized the gold? Could the party be successfully challenged as are the inmates of a coach on the heath? There was an interminable list of mights, and coulds, and ifs, and meanwhile, most tantalizingly, a few feet away, the gold chinked and the laughter of the careless players rang out. Now and then there were little disputes and one or other of the players would appeal to the man named Fielding.

Now, many things might have happened, but nothing then planned by the highwaymen did, for, by chance, one of a band of masked merrymakers came running, pursued in sport by another, and the runners stumbled on the hiding-place of Tom King and Dick Turpin. Had the two plotters remained where they were even then, all might have gone well, but, ever alert against discovery, they leaped to their feet and ran. As luck had it, at the same moment the heavily-built man named Fielding chanced to step out of the summer house and Tom King ran into his arms. Now, King was slight and active, but the big man was strong and suspicious too. Perceiving a couple of men running from cover with what seemed to be two in pursuit of them, he acted promptly and laid hold of the highwayman, calling meanwhile to those within to bring lights. But Tom King was hardy, keen and bright, and struggled vigorously.

"If you be an honest man, keep still until we have seen your face," roared Fielding as he took a firm grip of King's collar. "But if you are one of those thieving rogues who infest this place and London, then—"

The sentence was left unfinished, for Tom King gave a furious wrench and freed himself, leaving the collar of his fine coat in the big man's hands.

Things became confused then and the card-players shouted an alarm, while the maskers gathered near-by. Tom King, running with all possible speed, caught up with his companion, and the two of them made for a little group of trees some hundred yards away. The obscurity of the gardens aided them wonderfully, and it was much darker there. Beyond was an open space, lighted and dotted with people, who, having heard the

HIGHWAYMEN

outcry, stood staring and listening. The hunted men saw the rusty-looking man of the riverside inn, too, and he seemed to be going from group to group, and from each group there went up a cry of "Thieves are about!" That, indeed, was no new cry there. Night after night there had been trouble, and frequently footpads were caught, so that thief-hunting had almost become one of the expected sports. Just now people were more on the *qui vive,* for it had been rumored that highwaymen accustomed to haunt the roads north of London were in town, and rewards were out. Indeed, the hue and cry for Tom Palmer, *alias* Dick Turpin, had been over the town since the Dover coach was robbed, nearly six months before.

Not long did the highwaymen stay in the clump of trees, for half-a-dozen young fellows, eager for something new and exciting, advanced that way, and the two men made a dash for a row of bushes. They were at once seen and a great halloo went up, some giving cry like huntsmen. Having gained the hedge, King and Turpin made their way along it to a place where they thought it joined the boundary fence, only to find their cover stop short close to the edge of an ornamental pond.

Again they were seen and the air seemed to be at once full of noise, and lanterns glittered everywhere. To make matters worse, there came to their ears the sound of a trumpet, for Valentine Snow, musician and public favorite, had gotten wind of the man-hunt and was making merry with a fanfare. At one moment the coast seemed clear and they were about to make another dash, for their pursuers had no plan and hunted in groups and little bands, but other shadows, moving furtively, appeared, and they caught the flash of swords. So they crouched low and were like men caught in a torrent where everywhere was danger.

The sound of the trumpet caused the majority of the pursuers to gather in the quadrangle surrounding the orchestra, and, regaining their feet, the highwaymen could see, by the light of a thousand lamps, the steadily gathering crowd of men and women, the latter, with their great head-dresses of feathers and flowers, making a great ado in the summoning of their escorts. Here and there men were standing on seats and others on supper-tables addressing little knots of people, and it became clear that plans were being laid for systematic pursuit.

No time was lost then, and, making a swift dash, the highwaymen ran in the direction of what they thought was the Thames. Soon they came to a hedge fence where was an opening, crowded through, and, after a little indecision, turned sharply to the left, ran crouchingly under the cover of the vegetation, sped across a vacant piece of land that was almost a swamp, hit upon a gap in a board wall and discovered, on the other side a quiet and dark street. Two minutes later they were at the riverside and by merest chance came upon a boat boy who had a leaky wherry. They per-

suaded him to take them and, after much rowing, for
the tide was against them, were landed at Salisbury
Stairs. So, by back ways and alleys they reached the
corner of Drury Lane and Coal Street where, a few
doors away, stood Old Matthew's Inn. The house was
dark and the window shutters were up, but the highwaymen, after knocking in a peculiar manner and
giving, after challenge from within, a pass word, were
admitted. They found themselves in a room full of
hopeful striplings, of pickpockets, housebreakers and
dice-players and were immediately surrounded, heroes
for the moment.

The innkeeper, Old Matthew, a fat and red-faced
rascal, was none too pleased to see them, and his face
fell as he heard their tale. Nothing in his manner
invited them. Indeed, he was politely hostile.

"It is dangerous, I tell you," he said emphatically.
"I tell you, as I told that young fool, Jack Sheppard,
when he got out of Newgate and came here, that London is no place to hide in when Bow Street and Newgate get wind of you." There was the shaking of a fat
and warning forefinger and much head-nodding. He
pondered awhile, then added: "Fifteen year it is since
I told Jack that same thing, and I remember it as if
it was yesterday. And there is the hue and cry out, and
now Captain Hawk is wanted, too. It's dangerous, I
say, dangerous. Not that I'm the man at any time to
turn my back on a lad in trouble. Mind you that."
He paused again and seemed to be searching his mind

for some powerful argument, some suitable flower of speech, then, sitting on the head of a beer barrel he said dolefully, "The skies is very dark. The skies is very dark, I tell you, lads."

For a time there was a hubbub of talk, some advising this, some that, but soon Tom King called for wine and threw a gold coin on the table. Then he commanded attention by hammering on the table. "Here's a luck to us all—drink, everybody."

That created a pleasant diversion and the dark clouds conjured by old Matthew were soon forgotten.

—3—

All the next day Dick Turpin and Tom King lay in a rear room littered with empty barrels, household goods, smoked hams, discarded clothes, and all manner of depressing things. It was clear that there was to be no venturing abroad until the noise of the Vauxhall affair had quieted, for, without sufficient justification, as far as evidence was concerned, it was said that Dick Turpin was one of the men found in the gardens.

The day waxing late, both men grew impatient, nor were they any too trustful of their acquaintances in the face of the reward offered for their apprehension. The old innkeeper, they knew, would shelter them as long as he could with safety to himself, for he knew on which side his bread was buttered and many a guinea had he gained by the sale of watches and rings that the highwaymen had given him to dispose of. So towards evening, the grandson of Matthew, a shock-headed lad, was sent to the stables near Smithfield where their horses lay, and the two men made themselves ready for flight.

A little before eight that evening the horses arrived, both in the best of condition, Black Bess shapely and shining and snorting loudly, bravely set off with her handsome trappings. The eyes of Dick Turpin grew bright and shining when he saw his pet, and at once he began to tell Old Matthew the tale he had heard about Walpole who had ridden two horses to death. "My mare," he said, "would wear out twenty."

The two highwaymen were drinking a farewell glass with old Matthew, when there came to their ears the clatter of hoofs in the street. At the same moment a short, red-bearded man thrust his head in at the door and shouted that police officers were coming, then promptly disappeared. Cautiously the two robbers peered through the window, craning their necks to get a side glance, and caught sight of a little band riding that way. Behind the horsemen were many curious townsmen, at least a score, all keenly agog to know what was afoot. But the foremost rider had not reached the door before Tom King and Dick Turpin were again in the rear room, old Matthew with them, the tapster being left to attend to matters in the tap room.

From their hiding-place the three heard the confusion of noise and voices, and it was a little time before the words of one of the crowd came to them clearly.

"Without loss of time," he commanded, "let us know where this Dick Turpin is hidden. We are told that your master knows."

Then there was noise again and much calling for drink. The three in the dark back room were very quiet, and the old inn-keeper took down a picture that hung on the wall, so disclosing a peep-hole that revealed the bar-room. As he did so he signaled to the two to be silent.

"A tough crowd," he said hoarsely, speaking in the hollow of his hand. "And Lord, what a time! I am here at a most damnable risk to myself, for that they will search the house is not to be doubted."

"Some other way out there must be," suggested Turpin. "A cellar? A back door? The roof?"

"There is only one way out—the front way," was Matthew's answer.

"We might make a dash for it," said King.

"A pretty suggestion indeed," said Matthew. "Be trapped, you would, and this house battered about my ears. I remember all too well what was done to Jonathan Wild's house. But wait a while. Belike I can talk them over." With that, he went out into the tap room, and, at his appearance, the confusion grew wilder.

"Let us end the matter, Tom," said Turpin. "It is not likely that the old man can keep them long with all his wine and wit."

"But how?" asked King, very thoughtful and serious. "A bold dash? I am willing."

"There is the roof, and from one roof there is way to another. A risk, yes. But I would risk much for Black Bess."

The sound of many moving feet made them hasten, for it seemed evident that the excitement had spread and others from the street had entered. Like a trumpet blast they heard the voice of the officer in charge crying out that notwithstanding all that the inn-keeper said, the house would have to undergo a thorough search.

Lighting a candle then, which they carefully shaded, the two men sought the stairway, which was shielded by a door. This they bolted on the inside, and mounted the stairs to find themselves in a long, low room over the bar. It was a bedroom, and the window of it gave on the street. Opening the casement they looked down and saw that it was a drop of some fourteen feet to the cobblestones below, no great matter for light and active men. By the yellow light that shot through the window and open door of the inn they saw their horses on the other side of the street, tethered by their reins to an empty and horseless cart. The horses of the police officers· were grouped about the door below, stamping and snorting, and through the night came the swell of the voices.

As they looked, surveying the situation, they saw down the street, turning the corner from Long Acre, four mounted men, and it became clear that action must not be delayed. Further, there was plainly a change below, for doors were opening and slamming, and, at the foot of the stairway, men were thundering on the bolted door. Dick crawled out of the casement, hung a moment to the window ledge, then dropped into the street, his companion following close on his heels.

In spite of his sorry trade, Turpin was tall and straight and lean as a harrier, hardy, keen and bright, and no athlete could have crossed the street, released his horse, and leaped into the saddle quicker than he did. Black Bess gave a snort, and, without signal, broke into a canter. Dick supposed that his companion was equally lucky, but, turning as he rode to look at the horsemen coming from Long Acre, he was astonished to see that somehow Tom King's horse had slipped on the cobblestones and that the rider was on the ground, on hands and knees. Like a shot there leaped from the inn door a couple of the officers. One of them darted at Tom King, and the horse, startled, broke away and cantered towards the four horsemen. For a moment Dick Turpin meditated a rescue. He had, indeed, drawn his sword with the intention of charging at the officers. Seeing the rider thus, the bystanders fled precipitately, urging one another and looking over their shoulders as they ran. Highwaymen trapped had a reputation for recklessness.

Yet there seemed still a chance that Tom King might win to freedom, for he was wrestling with a man in uniform and was clearly the superior in agility. But another came running from the inn with sword upraised at a moment when King had gained his feet.

"Shoot, Dick, shoot!" called King, and the words were no sooner said than Turpin fired at the officer with the upraised sword. Perhaps in the uncertain light his aim was false and perhaps his mare swerved. Which it was Dick Turpin never knew and his heart fell when he saw his friend fall before the luckless shot. The rest was blotted out, for at the noise of the shot the houses vomited forth people and the little troop of horsemen dashed forward.

"Stand, Dick Turpin! You are prisoner!" roared an officer.

But the knight of the road was taking no chances. Pressing Black Bess with his knees and loosing her rein he bent low, fearing shots. Then the shrill sound of a whistle broke on his ears and pistols cracked. The canter became a swift gallop then, nor did he feel a measure of safety until Black Bess had the soft turf of Lamb's Conduit Fields under her hoofs, and, his pursuers nowhere in sight, he was riding up the almost imperceptible rise that led to Highgate.

—4—

You must figure him something of a dandy in a way, his mare, his cherished treasure, a creature of beauty and grace, his figure gay with buckskin breeches and spurred jack boots, his waistcoat of white satin and his coat of scarlet cloth, as he rides in the moonlight. To him a night ride meant nothing, for he knew the country well, and for years his way had led to quiet places where inns were far apart and roads not too well frequented, but well shadowed with tall elm trees.

At Highgate he turned, taking the road that led eastward, and so came to the village of Tottenham. Descending the road on the north of that settlement, a collection of not more than two dozen houses all darkened, he became aware of the clatter of hoofs behind him, and, turning, saw a little band of horsemen riding at full speed. At once he was filled with black forebodings, for he had supposed that his pursuers were thrown off the trail. Still there could be no mistake, for, as the horsemen came through Tottenham High Street, he heard the cry of "Stop, thief! Stop, thief!" At that he became convinced of his danger. The officers, he saw, must have split into parties, some taking one road, some another, and he had but lost time in his detour. Yet, with foolish daring, he gave a shout which the pursuers answered with a defiant yell, and a shot was fired at random. Then Dick Turpin shook his rein, and Black Bess broke into a rapid canter.

He laughed a little then, for the joy of the chase was in him and the steady beat of the mare's hoofs made him happy in spite of sorrow at his friend's death. Then, too, after the turmoil of the town, the gentle rustling of the leaves as the soft night air played with them was like music to his ears. About the men on his trail he troubled little, feeling that he could shake them off whenever he chose. Besides, Epping Forest was not far away. For the present, let Black Bess show her paces and tire those who followed.

A couple of miles farther he heard the sound of approaching men as he was descending a gentle slope. It was plain that travelers were on the road and coming towards him, but, also, his pursuers were on his heels and on either side of the road were tall hawthorn bushes through which it was impossible to press. Deciding quickly, he lightly pressed his mare, full of determination to meet matters boldly. Luckily for him there was a turn in the road so that he was not seen by those approaching until he was almost upon them. So it came about that he encountered them just as they were fording Palmer's Creek. No pause. No hesitation. At them he charged, calling on them to make way as he galloped, and this they did without objecting word or hampering hand. Indeed, the considerable splashing made by his mare as she dashed into the water aided him, for the riders, all unprepared for fight and on their way from Enfield to London, were careful of their clothes and at vast trouble to guard themselves from the leaping water-drops. So they merely shielded themselves as best they could, complaining loudly at the unseemly haste and discourtesy of the wild night-rider, and little thinking him to be a hunted man.

By all that, Dick Turpin was the gainer, doubly so

because when the Enfield men met the officers there was a halting to talk, the pursuers wanting to know whether the highwayman seemed to be making for Epping Forest and why so many had not stopped the fugitive.

Meantime, Dick Turpin had gained the clean, white town of Edmonton where stood the Cat and Bagpipes, an inn and ale-house well known to him. Ten miles he had ridden already and his mare was as fresh as when she stood in Drury Lane, nor was rider any whit the worse for the travel.

The sight of the inn gladdened him. In the moonlight it seemed to invite, with its red-curtained windows, its plank seat outside the door, its creaking swinging sign, the horse trough and tall elms, so that for a moment he regretted the chase.

At the sound of the approaching rider the ostler came from the stable and instantly recognized Dick. Many a gold coin he had received from Turpin and many an evening they had sat and talked of horseflesh. In the lad, Turpin noticed a new eagerness.

"There is no passage, Dick," said the lad. "That is, I am told to wake the house should you pass. So speed, Dick, speed, and good luck be with you."

"But why this haste?" asked Dick. "To-night I ride to Chingford, and there are those behind me who must be thrown off the scent."

Hearing that, the ostler became doubly insistent.

HIGHWAYMEN

"Not to Chingford," he said. "Captain Hawk is in danger. He stopped the mail coach and things went wrong, and now has gone to St. Albans."

He was interrupted from further explanation by the sound of the shrill whistle of the pursuing officers, at which noise the dogs of the neighborhood starting barking. Hearing the lad's words, Dick Turpin did some complicated thinking. The road to Epping closed, Hawk's house in the hands of the officers, the man himself all but captive, and Tom King dead: things were in parlous condition. Plainly, Turpin could not stay about London and to go by the way of St. Albans would mean the capture of Hawk. He pondered a while. Then, suddenly, there shot through his memory what the man had said about Walpole, whose name, it seemed, had become famous because he rode two horses to death to carry news to a king. He, Dick Turpin, could do better than the Norfolk squire. Then came the decision.

"Listen," he said. "Tell the men who follow me that I ride to York. If they care to follow, they will find me at the Black Prince Inn."

"But, captain, that is madness," insisted the ostler. "Four days the coach takes."

"Let that be so," answered the highwayman, warming to his boastful decision. "Let this rider Walpole learn that not a horse in all England can do what Black Bess does. See that you let them know."

His voice was hoarse with excitement, and by the light of the lantern the ostler saw his eyes shining as he leaned to stroke his mare's neck.

"Then go, and good luck," said he. "But there is no time to lose, for here they come."

What with the clatter of hoofs, the noise of the whistle and the barking of dogs, the villagers were awake and heads were thrust from windows, for Edmonton was not accustomed to strange noises when it was near ten of the night. Turpin arranged himself in the saddle and swallowed a pot of ale with noisy appreciation, but, in spite of the ostler's urging, did not move until the officers were within earshot. Then, standing in his stirrups, he made one of his dramatic flourishes, calling out to the men that Black Bess would show all England what could be done and that he would prove this Norfolk Walpole a very trifler. "And if any of you care to follow," he shouted, "see to it that you get new horseflesh, for though the beasts you ride have gone a mere ten miles, they will not carry you to Waltham Cross." There was a wave of his hand and he was gone.

One man, bolder than his fellows, rode after Dick Turpin a little way, and while the highwayman knew, yet he made no sign that he did, believing that the man's purpose was to note whether he turned off on the road that led to Chingford. He allowed the fellow to follow, seeing to it that he stayed well in the rear, for Turpin had no mind to put Black Bess in danger of a chance shot. Coming to a low stone wall hard by a great oak, he reined in his mare and stood until the officer was well within sound of his voice.

"You are a plucky fellow and hold your life lightly. But hear me. It is idle for you to follow except you have a horse as clean limbed as mine, for she will carry me to York. I'll show your Norfolk squires what an Essex horse can do! Talk of your Walpole who rode two horses to death!" Dick spat in disgust, for that Walpole's eminence was altogether due to the fact that he had accomplished a feat of horsemanship was fixed in his mind. Little he knew of statesmanship and diplomatic ability.

"Four days' coach ride to York," warned the man.

"Be it so," said Dick. "Black Bess shall do it to-night."

The man listened and thought a while. Then he said: "Dick Turpin, I knew you when you were a lad, and I am not the sort to see you run your head into a noose. Our officer is Skellum, and he has a warrant by which he may have fresh horses wheresoever he finds them, and it is not likely that your mare can outride twenty."

"That you shall see," boasted Dick.

"But it is madness and I mean you nothing but good," insisted the man. "Slip away to Suffolk and get in a farmer's smock until the smoke has blown away."

"For that, thanks," replied the highwayman. "But tell your fellows that I ride to York, and so farewell."

"One thing more," said the man. "If you are so set on your ride, remember that this side of Warmington, on Alconbury Hill, there is an inn and the ostler is Jack Holt, a good man and true. You may trust him and he will help a man at a pinch."

There was no more then, for the officer had stayed too long already for his own good, and he turned to rejoin his fellows. So away, then, went Dick Turpin and Black Bess, hoofs rattling merrily on the good road, the lift and swing of the mare filling the man with a joyful sense that he and the beast were one. Ten miles, twelve miles, London behind him and a long road and a quiet night ahead! In the man there was a glory in the strength of his mare, a vast pride in her speed, and he was swept with a whirlwind of fierce joy as he thought that what Black Bess did that night would be told and sung all over the countryside. So they sped under the thin moon, cautiously over marsh lands, fast where the turf was clean and soft. Thatched cottages and dark farmhouses swept past, haystacks and windmills leaped from shadow worlds into solidity, little streams and ponds and dark waters where frogs croaked came and went. But it was joy to ride, for the air was clean and the wind good to feel on cheek and lip, and the smell of the countryside was better than wine. It was good to ride when man and beast were as one and the rest of the world was sleeping, except for the blundering few that followed far behind.— If only this Walpole of Norfolk were there to see!

A touch of the spur and Black Bess rose to it

Up hill and down dale, past great estates and gray churches, through villages and hamlets, fording creeks and clattering over bridges! Through sleeping Langford they passed swiftly, pausing to rest a brief while beyond, and at the foot of the hill where crouched the village of Sandy. Carefully Dick rubbed his mare down, bathing her and using his satin waistcoat by way of brush, then on again, leaving the road to cut across the fields and so avoid a turn, coming again into the highway near St. Neots. Across the road was a turnpike gate and the keeper of it fast asleep. No matter. A touch of the spur and Black Bess rose to it, going over and landing light, as the nightcapped turnpike man came to his door, shouting for his toll. Straight, then, to Huntingdon and through the High Street. Ninety-nine miles done and the mare going strong at the end of six hours' ride. The hoarse crowing of the cocks on the outskirts of town sounded like trumpetings of victory to the rider, and when, hard by the market-place, he saw a watchman with lantern and stout stick, he had to draw rein sufficiently long to tell that fellow that he had ridden from London, and York town would be his journey's end. "See to it," he shouted, as he trotted off again, "that news gets to that fellow Walpole that at three in the morning I was in Huntingdon."

From Huntingdon to Alconbury Hill no great speed was made, and Dick nursed his mare carefully, though with no doubt as to the final outcome. Halting a while in a wood of oak trees whose wealth of light spring green seemed touched to silver, the highwayman chanced to see, away on the hilltop, two yellow lights, and then suddenly remembered the name of Jack Holt, ostler at the Inn of the Golden Goose. Thereupon he mentally blessed the police officer and made his way through Little Stukeley, walking and leading the mare. Arrived at the inn he saw that every one there was still abed, though the leaping color and light of a fire in the waiting room gave him the hope that the man he sought was afoot somewhere, alert and active.

When Jack Holt did appear, which was as soon as he heard the horse, he was all for saddling and bridling a fresh horse speedily, thinking the rider to be some belated wayfarer in haste, well supplied with money, for it was rare indeed that riders came at that time of night or early morning. When he heard how matters stood and that Dick had ridden from London, the fellow could not do too much, be the rider a highwayman or one on a king's errand. His grandfather, he said, had befriended Captain Hind, the Gentleman Knight of the Road, and he himself had once seen Claude Duval, so he came honestly, he suspected, by his admiration for Dick Turpin of whom he had heard. Meanwhile, he was not idle. With warm water from the kitchen he bathed Black Bess and no mother could have been more gentle. As he worked, when he was not talking in his broad, north-country accent, he kept up a low hissing, though when he detected a little swelling above a hoof, he dropped into a kind of low moaning.

Yet the while he was quick and nimble. But it was a rare miracle that he worked, for, in a very short while, the mare was whinneying softly and nosing the hay, comfortable in a stall and covered with a blanket. So, all things about the mare being made orderly, the good Jack Holt did what might be done for the rider, bringing him food and drink, the which was sorely enough needed. That being done, he made a clean bed of straw near the stall in which Black Bess rested and bade Dick rest a while, telling him that with the early morning must come travelers. As for Dick, being so weary, he was soon like a man dead, nor did he know that he slept until he felt a light hand on his face.

"Now you must slip out quietly," said Holt. "The officers are coming from London way and you have slept a little short of an hour. But I will show you a way by following which you may gain much time."

Dick was on his feet at once and a moment later had the mare saddled and the reins over the crook of his arm. Then Jack Holt led him to the rear of the stable which, as he then saw, was perched on the crest of a hill, the front of it facing the inn, the rear giving sharply on a place so steep as almost to be precipitous. It was a tall bluff rather than a hillside, a bluff dropping so straight that it seemed as though a goat would hardly find foot-hold. At the bottom of it, looking like a mass of bushes, lay Walton Woods, and faintly, by the gray light, could be seen a white, winding road.

"Lead your mare down there," said Holt, "and if

she is as sure-footed as she seems to be, and if you do not grow giddy, you will save at least three miles. The officers must change horses and doubtless also eat. And if I can I will send them by way of Peterborough while you take the road to Warmington. So good luck to you."

There was no more then, for, guided by Holt, Dick led the mare out by way of four stone steps, and the stable door was closed on man and mare. It was none too soon, for through the deadly still of the early morning came the ring of horses' hoofs nearer and nearer. Straining his ears, the highwayman could sometimes hear the clang of scabbards on iron stirrups.

A long time seemed to pass in dread and in watchfulness as horse and man descended the dangerous hill. A slip at any time would have brought confusion or death upon them, a loose stone might mean an early end. Soon, Dick had to throw the reins over the mare's neck, leaving her to pick her own way, for with his jack boots and spurs he was in far sorrier straits than the beast. But Black Bess went, delicate as a cat, now daintily stepping, now sliding on her haunches, and she was on level ground before her master, who, towards the last, somehow lost his footing and went rolling, saving himself by clutching at bushes.

At Warmington the world began to wake. Farmers' lads and early milkmaids looked up from their work to see the strange rider, and there were hubbubs in chicken yards and the barking of dogs as they passed. There was more noise in the market place and much shouting, for the strange-looking rider was something new to the early men who had come with their pigs and sheep and cattle for market day. Those in the street who saw, rushed into the inn and to houses to tell others, and so there was confusion. Trying to avoid the market place in which there were too many, though the morning was yet so young, Dick turned down a side street, people flocking fast on his heels in astonishment. Then he saw that he had made a mistake, for the street was narrow and at the lower end of it was a man with a low market cart to which was harnessed a donkey and the fractious beast had backed in such manner that the cart stood across the street, blocking the way from house to house. Through the gap of houses Dick saw beyond the clean white country road with trees on either side, an arcade of green. At the barrier went the highwayman and fire flew from the stones as Bess leaped. Over cart and donkey she flew, the little man, who was hot and hatless, waving his arms furiously. So, clear of the town at a leap, as it were, they passed into the open again and along a ridge, on either side of which was wide, free country, plowed land and grass land and fields bordered with high elms bearing countless rooks' nests.

Straight over the low, flat-topped hill to Fineshade Abbey went horse and rider and already in the valley faint wisps of mist began to rise. Past the abbey lands they went, over the boulder-strewn water course and up on to the ridge, the rough top of which was softened by ferns and moss, leaving the winding road again to cut across an untilled piece of heather land, into a stretch of timbered country and so to Stamford, where Dick dismounted for a short while and Black Bess nibbled the grass, all fragrant and cool because of the dewfall.

An unpleasant surprise awaited him, for when he remounted, it became clear that the gallant mare was tiring. But still she kept on bravely, though the lilt and the spring were gone out of her stride. The plunge into the cold water when they crossed the Trent, for they forded at a pebbly place and the water was deeper than it looked, left the mare plainly weaker. Still, with the caressing warmth of the sun, she pulled together wonderfully and there were miles when she went at a rapid trot. No Tartar stallion could have bested her, no Arab desert horse shown more endurance.

Up hill and down dale, then, and along a hard, rough road shut in by low hedges, they went, and Black Bess grew heavy-hoofed; but at Thorne, some early morning rider came from a side lane mounted on a stout cob and there was a change. Up went the ears of Bess and there was a new energy in her and her hoofs beat with a steady thud again as she strove to overtake her fellow. In her veins was new life, in her sinews new strength, and she snorted in a moment of exaltation as she went for a while side by side with her rival, then passed him.

At the milestone that read
YORK
15 M.
weariness and exhaustion seemed to come upon the mare suddenly. One moment she was moving, pluckily, heavily, then of a sudden, she was down in a heap. There was one struggle to regain her feet and that was all. Close by, a brook ran through the meadow and Dick Turpin staggered to the water, bringing back some in his hat, but he saw that it was useless and that there was no hope. One moment he stared stupidly, then he was rent with a whirlwind of passion that ended in sobs. Thief and robber, caring for nothing that most men hold dear, yet there was in him an unsuspected love for his mare, a fullness of soul until then unknown. He lifted her head, looked into her glazing eyes, lovingly patted her neck, spoke to her; then he drew away and stood in the road gazing at the strange black heap that was once arched neck and rounded flank and glossy mane. Something had gone out of the world for him. The sweetness of the new day, the murmur of the wind in the grass, the song of the lark in the air—all these he was conscious of only as things in a dream world. The only real thing seemed to be there in the yellow dust of the road.

Presently he set off towards York, walking mechanically, a travel-stained figure with bent head. But not far did he go. He turned and retraced his steps, walking slowly until he reached the strange heap that was once Black Bess. Then he sat by her side on a stone and there those who pursued found him.

* * * * * * * *

There is, on the desk before me as I write, an old woodcut of the execution of Dick Turpin at York Castle, and the date of the event is given as April 10th, 1739. With the artist, it was probably necessary to bear in mind the habit of hero worship. At any rate, as the crowd is pictured standing about the gallows tree, there is but one prepossessing face. Dick Turpin alone is handsome and debonaire as he stands on the fatal ladder in his finery, attired in fine laced coat and highly polished jack boots, a flower at his breast. The hangman is plainly a villain and ugly to excess. The sheriff who stands on the overcrowded execution platform has the face of a demon, and the attendant minister of the gospel, who is pictured as a bishop arrayed in full canonicals, has about him an air of cynical levity. As for the military—apparently the British army in the days of King George the Second was composed of Calibans.

According to the popular account, Dick Turpin's manner of going to his death was marked by dramatic distinction. His passing was a remarkable achievement. Though "under the influence of a drug," yet at the last moment there came from him "a burst of scornful laughter at the irony of fate," and, "at the moment when the sea of faces and the other varied objects around faded from before Dick's eyes, yet there was no quailing in that last glance." And the woodcut shows that plainly. The highwayman's features are stern but pleasant, his manner noble and easy, his bearing frank and unashamed. The law, as typified in the sheriff, is obviously vindictive and brutal. With fine spiritual insight, according to the popular mythology, the highwayman would not allow death to be meted out to him at the hands of a common hangman, and "no sooner had the hangman spoke the word, than, with a sudden bound, the Prince of Highwaymen threw himself off the ladder. . . . And so, bold and defiant to the last, the gallant Dick Turpin met his fate."

CLAUDE DUVAL

*"Taught the wild Arabs of the road
To rob in a more gentle mode;
Take prizes more obligingly than those
Who never had been bred filous;
And how to hang in a more graceful fashion
Than e'er was known before to the dull English nation."*
—Butler.

CLAUDE DUVAL

KINGS are kings, and pages are pages, and in the round dance of life they mix and mingle and it sometimes comes to pass in the hurly-burly that page catches sight of the truth that behind the mask and trappings of a king there stands a man, though it is more rare that a king realizes that a man may hide in the silk and ruffles of a page. Now, of all kings, Charles II had many and strange adventures, made many discoveries of men, and one he found, most unexpectedly, in the year 1664, and this is the tale of it:

One summer day the king walked forth at Whitehall to look at his bees, having caused posts to be set for new hives, and being curious to see how they did in their new homes. For old Rowley, though strong and burly, with harsh and saturnine expression and rough, booming voice, yet loved the things of Nature and saw much to admire in the dewdrops, the quiet meadows and the fleecy clouds. So, having tired of the bees, he fell to playing with his dogs on the Whitehall lawn, and, had he been stripped of his finery and dressed in homespun, those who saw, not knowing him, might have taken him for some garden laborer.

Not far off, under the shade of an elm tree, sat a court page, one named Claude Duval, who had been brought to the Court from France, and, having nothing better to do and being out of hearing of the king, he took his flageolet and fell to playing. He was a tall young fellow, clear of skin and straight as a spear, and, though amorous of countenance as the English counted things, yet his eyes were keen and there was the glint as of steel in them, so that in many respects he was far from the sort one might look to see dangling at the heels of courtiers or dancing attendance upon beribboned ladies. Indeed, but for the fact that his salary was far in arrears and that my lord Roper had promised him payment did he but have patience, he would have left to fight the Dutch long before. So, happy enough at heart, but full of thought, he played his music, a new tune by Master Pelham Humphreys, and was so enwrapped with the melody that he did not see the king, who, having tired of his dogs, had drawn near and stood in the gateway listening, nodding his head to the lilt of it.

"A merry tune, young man," he said gayly when the music had ended, and Claude Duval, recovered from his surprise, made obeisance. The king went on, "See to it that you get the air pricked down so that my fiddlers may play it." Then, with a lapse into a certain rough humor, he said, with the veiled gladness of one to whom has come a pretty thought, "Music, I hold, is better than gold. Gold you may hold, you may gaze on a while, and, whiff! it is gone. The joy of it cannot be pricked down. In truth, there is no joy in it until it is given into the hand of another. But music, that is a different thing. I mind the words of that fellow, Richard Edwards, who wrote:

> O, music! whom the gods assigned
> To comfort man, whom cares would nip!
> Since thou both men and beast doth move,
> What beast is he, will thee disprove?

'Twas well said indeed. Gold itself is a care that doth nip, the want of it a greater care. So I say, Music is better than gold."

Hearing all that, Claude Duval pulled a long face, and, to the king's notion, looked so sad, yet so comical in his puzzlement, that the king burst into a hearty roar.

"Why, truly, page," said he, "I see no merriment in your face. What a sorry Orpheus have we! Is it the sadness of love? Some maid of honor?" There was an explosion of boisterous merriment again.

"I was thinking, your majesty, of what you said, and the truth of it shadowed me. For you said that you held music to be better than gold." This was said a little wistfully.

"A trifle: a mere conceit that leaped to mind," said the king in high good humor. "Herrick might weave a song about such a remark."

"Still, music, like other things, sire, thrives better with the nourishment that gold gives," said Claude, and paused a while as if wondering whether it would be wise to say more. But suddenly his backbone was stiffened and he looked the king in the eyes. "Truth is, your majesty, I have lived long on mere promises and somewhat eaten the air of hope, lining myself on promise of supply, as—"

"Hoity-toity!" growled the king, with his blackest frown. "Is a king never to talk without being plagued with money matters? Nor, by my faith, is that a pretty speech for a page!"

"Nor are promises pretty pay for a man," retorted Duval hotly, flinging diplomacy aside, and, at the words, a dangerous flush swept the swarthy face of the monarch. For a moment he stabbed the page with a stare, his eye kindling with swift anger; then another mood swept over him.

"'Od's fish!" said he. "We hear strange things in these days. Time was, young man, when fellows of so lively a tongue had their ears clipped and their prettiness spoiled for less. But the world, it seems, grows kinder or slacker, I know not which."

He growled and rumbled like a distant summer storm, then turned on his heel, snapped his fingers to his dogs and took a stride or two away. But he stopped

HIGHWAYMEN 123

and laughed, speaking from the little distance, and said:

"I am in mood to hear you talk, young fellow. I have seen you about the place and often thought you far too bold in appearance for a court page. Your name, sirrah?"

"Claude Duval, sire, of the Duvals of Domerey," was the reply.

"Ha! Then, page, I am minded to think aloud, talking and hearing freely, for, by heaven, it is rare enough that I can pass the invisible wall that is built about a king. Yet there was a time, after Worcester, when I met many good men and rough, plain-speaking men, and to me the wonder of it was that they went to such a coil of trouble for me. But at court it is rare to meet a man. The most of them are masks, shadows of men with their 'ohs' and their 'ahs', do I but look at a thing; slippery rascals they, forever on the lookout for their own advantage. So bold a rascal as this Penn comes but once in a season—beshrew me! The man came before me and kept his hat on his head, calling me Friend Charles. That he did. 'Twas then that I put off mine, saying that 'twas the custom of the place that but one at a time should be covered. Ah! but there's savor to such a man. Then there is that bear Hobbes, too. But for the rest, dancing ninnies, sycophants. The foxes they, telling me forever to ask the Houses for money, and, I doubt not, going to this one and that at Westminster whispering and plotting to checkmate me. A flock of cackling geese, a bevy of peacocks are these courtiers and hangers-on, and well minded am I at times to cast the whole burden aside. Indeed, 'tis but a folly and the ship will sail well enough without its figurehead."

Hearing all that, in Claude Duval's eyes there was the alert look of a man listening to something entirely unexpected, for that the king had troubles of that sort had not occurred to him.

"I had not dreamed, your majesty, that things were in such plight," he said, earnestly.

"Even so it is, Duval," said the king, showing his teeth in a grin. "You, a youth of twenty or so, sound and stout and whole, are far more free than I who, after all, am but a thing cage-cooped. This one and that counts his duty to talk for me, to think for me, to act for me, to arrange for me and, at the back of talking and thinking and acting, each has his own motive. Cabals and unions, plottings and plannings, and on my shoulders is this and the other laid. It should not be 'A king can do no wrong,' but 'A king can do no right.' Do I but read a book of verses, there is the fellow Dryden with his serious visage telling me I should read some other thing. And here is my Lord North, keeper of the king's character, and Burnet with his churchly discipline, and Rupert the madman with his plans, and Temple with his foreign affairs. 'Od's blood! They marry me, they feed me, they advise me and they prevent me. The Houses give me no money and the religious men no peace. So what though I be

HIGHWAYMEN

the first Briton born to wear three crowns, if no crowns jingle in my strong box?"

He fell silent then for a while, lifting a finger to call attention to the sweet crooning of some near-by doves; then, the soft voices ceasing, he went on, with a note of peevishness.

"Would that there were more Penderells in the world, for when I was fleeing after Worcester, more than half-dead from mere weariness, true men of mettle they proved themselves. And now, having the throne they helped me to, I lack a few guineas for a private business that the world needs to know nothing of."

Hearing that, blushing for the boldness of what he said, Claude spoke, saying, "If your majesty will but command me, I will bring to you by hook or by crook, the gold needed for that special business of which you speak. For I tire of doing nothing and sitting like a tame cat, and gladly will I risk a tussle with the master of the exchequer if need be. Sire, write down your command and give me a couple of men-at-arms and there is no gate so strong but I will force against odds, no treasury guardian so churlish but will yield to my persuasion. To be commanded is a favor I ask." So saying, he dropped to his knee.

The king pondered, plucking at his lip, then bade the page arise.

"Much need, but little hope, Claude Duval of Domerey," he said. "Still, it pleases me to see that all about the court are not men of straw. But certain things are now afoot and I look to France for some relief in the matter of money. But how it will all come to end I know not. Would that I had the crystal of Doctor Dee to peer into the years."

Hearing that, Claude Duval's face went red as fire.

"Your majesty—" he began and stopped short.

"Well," said the king, who, having said his say, seemed to have grown tired of his mood and grown impatient.

"As to telling the future, sire, there is in town a certain doctor who—"

"Doctor me no doctors," laughed the king, turning away as if to go.

"Yet this, sire, is a strange man from Germany of repute and one who has told odd things with crystal balls, seeing in them things clear as the sun at noonday. He is skilled in the arts of Nixon and of Shipton and of Wakefield, the last who by similar means told of the end of King John."

"Of Wakefield I have read something in the chronicles of Grafton, but I place small faith in it," said the king.

"But, your majesty, this man foretells many things and some have already come to pass. Many of the court go secretly to his house, which is but a stone's throw from the Pindar near to Bagnigge Wells."

"Tells he aught of interest other than that a man shall meet a maid, that a man shall come to great wealth and so on, which, indeed, is the way of these fellows of small imaginings?"

"Yes. He does, your majesty. When, a month or so past, five were said to have died of the plague in Coal Lane, he foretold that, within a year, sixty thousand in London town would die of the same distemper."

"A sorry madman he," observed the king.

"Another strange thing," continued Claude. "He has said that the plague would continue until fire fought it, and with that fire the half of London would be burned. Also, he said, the Dutch would sail into the Thames and burn English shipping."

"A Cassandra, this fellow," growled Charles.

The page seemed to be anxious to push his story. "In France," he went on, "this doctor made magic philters whereby men were made to love women so that Mme. Montespan is said by such means to have preserved the king's affections."

"That indeed is a gift," laughed Charles. "Would that I had some such powders." He stole a glance at Duval and waited a moment, then added in a kind of parenthesis, "Now were you a proper courtier you would tell me that I need none such, hinting that the affections of women were mine for the wish. Howbeit, it is certain that Louis of France gazes at the diamond-bedecked madam with far more devotion than at his altar, and her husband, who hath wit enough, inveighs loudly against the king's friendship for her."

After that there fell a silence, the king seeming to be in deep thought. Suddenly, without turning, he said:

"A pest on many things. Should I go to see this doctor of whom you speak, not one, but a hundred craning necks would be stretched and twice that number of ears would be at walls. Our good Master Evelyn would be writing of it in his daily book. Burnet, too, would be biting his pen, thinking how best to set it down in black and white. Nor would Clarendon be slow in telling it here and there, and if not Otway, then Rochester, would be making verses about it. *Ma foi!* I cannot speak a private word but the court is set a-buzzing and there are whispering tongues to poison truth, and half lies and tittle-tattle in corners. Many, too many, are the guardians of our blood and state, Claude Duval.— But here comes D'Urfay. Not a word. See to it that you manage quietly and bring or send this necromancer to me. If he knows France and the court and Louis, as you say, there may be things that he can tell. E'en lacking that, it will be sport and relief from a yawning court."

So there was no more of that, and the page made his low bow and was about to withdraw when the king halted him.

"Remember, as I said, music is better than gold. Yet, I do heartily wish that a lad of mettle, stout for his inches as you, had the power to transport Midas as easily as you win Apollo."

—2—

The necromancer's house stood in a sun-bright, flower-filled garden, musical with the loud humming of honey-seeking bees and the white walls of his dwelling were almost covered with a mass of greenery besprinkled with crimson roses, while wide staring hollyhocks guarded the gravel walk.

The old man, a dark-eyed, sallow-skinned figure in a long silken robe, heard Claude Duval's message gravely, sitting the while perfectly still. At the end, making a polite gesture, he told the page that a king's wish was a command. So, there being nothing else left to do and his mission ended, Duval took his leave. But before he reached the garden gate, the old man halted him with a quizzical expression.

"A moment, young sir," he said in a soft voice. "And have you no curiosity? Have you no desire to know what fate holds in store?" He peered up at Duval and held out an arresting hand, a hand that trembled slightly with a nervous movement.

Duval laughed a little. "Soon I shall be making my own way and fortune, for I cannot dangle about a court all the days of my life."

"That need not be said," put in the old man, and so swiftly on the heels of what Claude himself had said, that all seemed part of a single sentence. "It is not hard to see. A youth of merit, clean and bright-eyed, of valor, of ambition, one whose world is a world of ease and plenty, must, perforce, do something. But what? The wars? To sail to the western land? To fight the Dutch?"

Claude Duval's indifference had vanished. Seeing his condition thus sketched lightly he was interested in spite of himself. "What?" he asked.

The old man shrugged his shoulders. "To live, one works or one steals, by whatsoever name the stealing is called, and much that is called work is but robbery tricked out in strange disguise. You are not the sort to roughen your hands with honest toil, but neither are you the sort to dangle at court. So if you do not labor, you must steal."

"You talk in riddles," said Duval. "If your mood is pleasantry, I like it little."

The old man chuckled. "To labor or to steal, young sir, though stealing hath many names. As for your court duties, a fig for them! They hold you less than a silken thread. Say you flatter yourself that you honor your king, it is, after all, but a love for yourself. All men hide their self-love under some cloak or other. As for your cloak, finding it a threadbare one, an unworthy one, you will cast it aside. And then? What then? Will you, knowing only a world of idle men and luxury, seek a life among those that toil in squalor and ugliness? No. Ease and a modicum of power you have had, and that same will you seek."

"Is this then a sample of your foretelling?" asked Claude.

"It is," was the answer. "I do but note the way things go, then tell men the direction, those who hear me dressing up the thing said in empty words. So."

"It was not thus with your tale of a plague," persisted Claude. "There indeed was no direction, as you are pleased to call it."

"A plague is no new thing," said the old man. "Here there is filth, and with filth cometh sickness. Men do not learn by their experience. Less than thirty years ago in this very city thirty thousand were slain by it, and ten years before that went ten thousand more than that by the same cause. At Lyons in France, sixty thousand fell before it some thirty years ago. How rats carry it I know not, but certain it is that when rats come in great numbers, there is a foretelling of the plague. You see, my page, the gods play with men and these things are their games. I do but remember the sport the gods have had, and foretell of more sport of a like nature, for the gods are of small imagination."

"A strange tale," said Claude thoughtfully. "Yet it seems to bring you no scanty living."

He said this as a liveried man of very sober aspect whom the old man called Solomon Eagles, brought in a tray of delicate wood-carving on which was a bottle and some cakes. The tray he set on a bench without saying a word, then went his way again. The necromancer picked up the bottle, which was of blackish glass, and started to pour out a little white wine, then, suddenly lifted the neck of the bottle, saying: "But perhaps you prefer red wine, or canary wine."

"Red wine, an it please you," answered Claude, "but it is no great matter," not wishing to place a burden on his host, but telling truthfully his preference. To his immense astonishment, from the same bottle from which had been poured white wine came wine ruby red, and, his glass having been filled, the old man poured for himself and still from the same bottle, a glass of white wine. At that Claude's jaw dropped.

"A sweet pear," said the old man, and seemed to pluck one from the air. Seeming not to see Duval's astonishment, he went on, saying:

"He is indeed luckless who discourses of his own disability. Still, not from things that should count as of worth and that I tell men, do I gain my living. To such, men pay but small heed, alas. There is that matter of the Dutch. I know, very well, how the men of Holland look upon their fleet and admiral with pride and how they hate the English. It is also clear that the English care little for the welfare of their fleet, talking large of things that have been done by their forefathers. It is to be seen, then, that trouble must come, and soon. But telling that, I suffer indignity, for nations, like people, love the praise that stinks, hating the spur that drives to effort. No. No. I live by men's narrower interest. Let me tell you, young sir, that men are fools and credulous to a grave fault. To me comes this one and that for the philosopher's stone; another for the gift of changing lead into gold; another for love philters; another for the water of beauty; another for the spirit of the goat, and for these follies they pay with no niggard hand. It is a world without sense and the greatest fools are those who dream that they can change it."

Claude Duval's eyes looked frankly at the old man. "You are a rascal then," he said.

"If he is a rascal who works not at an honest trade, yes," answered the old man. "But observe well, I do but add glamour to crime, if crime it is to cheat in a new way those who seek to be cheated. For men speak well of the trimming and forget the garment and so it was ever. All this I tell because you are frank, and he who is frank with the frank learns much. So something I would gather from you of the king, of his character, of his doings. I ask no betrayal of secrets, for you are of the sort that has learned to keep close lips where need calls. But the truth you may give, and, when I see the king I will but tell him of himself, showing him the man he is, instead of the man he wishes to be thought. Fairer than that no man can say."

So there was an hour in which there was talk, and new horizons opened for the alchemist when he learned of the king's sore lack of money, of the way in which he was surrounded by those who sought to use him for their own purpose, and even of the disposition of the rooms and the very furniture of the place, for the old man seized upon all things, no matter how small. On his part, Claude laughed most heartily when he learned that the Duke of Orrery sought from the old man an elixir by means of which he might stay young; that Sir Richard Able wanted a charm by which he could excel in music and singing and dancing, and, above all, he found it amusing that the Duke of Ramsay would fain learn the alchemic art so that he, although a rich man and easily beyond want, might learn how to turn iron to gold. "Yet so it is," said the old man, "and this blessed night and in this house the duke will work like a slave at the crucible, he bringing the gold, I supplying the salt and the lead." The man's eyes twinkled merrily when he said this, and he added, as he laid a slight hand on the page's knee, "And if there be others in the court of like mind, those who would learn transmutation, tell them, good Claude Duval, that I am a student of the hermetic philosophy. Tell them that I have the secrets of Zachire, and of Dr. Dee, and of Cornelius Agrippa. Nor will it be to your disadvantage."

Claude left the place after that, telling the old man that what he had heard was good tidings. "Yet," said he, "some things that you have told are hard of belief. There is the Duke of Ramsay, for example, a man close-fisted enough, whose long face always led me to think that he did daily penance and wore a hair shirt. The tale told, that you have entrapped him, leaves me well content."

"So it is," said the old man. "Gold he seems to have

aplenty in spite of his long face, though to be sure it is with groans that he gives it and not with any sort of pleasantry."

After Claude's departure, the old man betook himself again to his garden and his roses, planning how he would use the new knowledge that he had gained in his interview with the king. But that night he waited long for the Duke of Ramsay to come with his gold, and when midnight came and no pupil, he began to fear that he had been too free with the page who, in the light of his knowledge had warned the duke; for with all his art and insight the necromancer little guessed what had taken place.

—3—

From the old man's house, Claude Duval went straight to the Royal Mews and, from the Duke of York's stable chose a swift horse, telling the stable boy that he would ride a while in the park. But there was no park for him. Instead, he rode out by way of Islington at a round pace, stopping only when he reached a place where the road which ran sharply up hill, wound in among trees. There he dismounted to wait, for that place the Duke of Ramsay must pass if the old man had spoken true as to his coming.

It was a place of vantage, for from it he could see, through a parting in the trees, a straight stretch of road to the gates of the Ramsay mansion, a red brick building behind which clustered a dozen little cottages. It was well for Claude Duval that he came thus early, for, had he been very little later, all would have fallen out otherwise. As it was, he had not been there long and the sun had scarce dropped below the horizon when the sound of horses' hoofs burst on his ears and a coach dashed past and gained considerable lead before Claude knew, by the uniform of the coachman and the servant on the box beside him, that it was his intended quarry. In an instant Duval had whipped a black mask across his eyes and was in the saddle and clattering down the road.

The five hundred yards that separated him from the coach was soon passed and Claude bounded on, past coach and horses. Then suddenly he turned, having gone far enough as he judged, and drew rein. At the same moment he put a little whistle to his lips and blew a shrill blast. At the sound the driver pulled up short and the man in the coach put out his head. Out came Duval's pistol then and, seeing it, the coachman threw up his elbow to shield his face while his fellow servant, a mere lad, sat open-mouthed.

"Now mark!" said Claude, stoutly enough. "Down, both of ye and cast loose the horses, taking them up the hill a good way. Nor move again until I blow the whistle."

"What would ye? What would ye?" called the nobleman in the coach, thrusting his head through the window. "What have ye in mind to do? Drive on, fellows, and that fast, nor heed this jackanapes."

"Back to your shell!" shouted Claude Duval, flourishing the pistol. "You and I have a little business to settle. And you, man, heed him not, but go as I said, except you value not your hides."

"Stand off!" called the duke, frowning formidably and showing his sword. "A highwayman! A rogue! A thief! Take heed, fellows, and attend to me and your business."

But the men had no mind for danger. The startled horses, high-strung and mettlesome, gave them enough to do, and they themselves were eager enough to be well away and out of danger. So, in short time, they had the horses clear of the coach and were leading them away to the cover of a clump of trees where they could see but not be seen, and knew themselves to be out of pistol range.

"Your gold, and quickly!" said Claude to the duke. "Also hold your clattering tongue for I have many things to do."

"I carry no money with me," said the duke, suddenly dropping his head like a man borne down with a weight of care.

"You lie, man," said Claude. "Well I know. And well can you spare the gold that you have, seeing that one who is within an ace of changing iron to gold has the riches of the world in his hand." For all his bold words there was a kind of pity in Claude Duval's heart.

"What is that? What is that?" asked the duke sharply. "Iron changed to gold, you say?"

"Those who empty crucibles near Bagnigge Wells without looking well to the result have small use for gold," said Claude.

In the dim light, Claude could see the pallor of anxiety on the duke's face and he pressed his point. "Small good will your new-found secret serve you though, for, in a minute you are a dead man lest you hang your bags of gold over my saddle. So haste, if you be not a born fool to risk your carcass."

As he spoke, Claude Duval pulled the lock of his pistol and the duke plainly heard the click. So there was no more hesitation and the nobleman stepped from his coach lugging two leather sacks with him, and, aided by the robber, threw them across the saddle. Yet he did not lack a proper spirit. His natural complexion had returned and he stood, boldly enough, at Claude Duval's knee, shaking a clenched fist.

"Jackanapes!" he said. "I'll rid the road of such vagabonds. A parcel of idle fellows who steal forth at night like carrion to rob and to pill. The land must soon be purged of your like and time cannot be long ere a good rope shall be your portion, my fine lad." His voice grew shriller with anger at the last, but having said his say, he turned and went back to his coach, too proud to move fast though he knew that the pistol was cocked.

But Claude was in high spirits, his task being done, and he laughed aloud. "Not yet a while, my lord duke," he said, and, giving his horse the rein, clattered away.

Nor did he stop until he was well up the hill towards London, when he took his whistle and gave a shrill blast to let the men know that he had done his business so that they could return to their fuming master.

• • • • • • • •

The stable boy knitted his brows when Claude returned with the horse, for it was nigh on midnight and the animal was sweating. But remark he made none, for Claude, having dismounted and slapped with hearty kindness the neck of the horse, dropped a fistful of gold into the lad's hand. Later, like golden keys gave him easy entry to the Duke of Richmond's house where, as he knew, the king was at cards. Indeed, with pockets lined with gold, many difficulties vanished. After a little waiting he was received by the king in an anteroom, his majesty privately wondering what strange new business was afoot. Flushed with pride and his success, Claude Duval laid his bag of gold at the king's feet, begging its acceptance.

"Oy, oy!" exclaimed the king, in vast astonishment and good humor. "What manner of man is this who brings gold instead of taking it? And why? For it is a new thing if you ask not more than you bring. Is it some place at court?"

"I ask nothing, sire," answered Claude. "This morning your majesty spoke of the Penderells who once had the good fortune to serve you. A like opportunity I crave. But there is more. Your wish was that I might find means to transport Midas as well as I could win

Apollo. So I have found Midas and persuaded him, and these, his gifts, I lay at your feet."

"*Ma foi!*" said the king, laughing. "It begins to look as though it was high time that there was a vacancy in the ranks of the court pages and, at the same time, a vacancy in the ranks of created knights. If your old German doctor will but prophesy concerning you as Sir Claude, that saying will I make come to pass."

Claude reddened with pleasure at that, and, with a great laugh, the king turned away, carrying the bag of gold with him.

—4—

The vacancy in the ranks of the pages came soon enough, but the knighthood that came to Claude was self-induced and not the gift of the king, and this was the way of it:

On the day following, the king and a few of his court were to attend the Duke's Theater where was being played "The Rivals," a thing patched up by Master Davenant from Fletcher's play, "The Noble Kinsman." As the play in those days commenced at three in the afternoon and after the hour of dining, many who attended were wine-witty and bottle-bold, so, to be out of the way of them, Claude Duval sat in a corner close to the stage, having his place in the pit, by virtue of his court rank, among the beaux of the town and the wives of well-to-do men, though none of the latter he

"So I have found Midas and persuaded him"

knew because of the vizards they wore in the fashion of the time.

The building was open to the sky, except over the stage, and the street cries and noises mingled with those within. One by one, calling "Oranges! Will you have any oranges?" the fruit girls entered, each with her basket of vine-leaf covered oranges. Lining themselves on the floor in front of the stage they offered their wares with a kind of brigandage, picking out a man here and there and challenging him to buy at a set price. Nor did any refuse, for to have done so or to have bargained was considered beneath the character of a gentleman. The oranges having changed hands became missiles soon, for the noisier of the gallants in the pit exchanged witticisms not alone with the orange girls, but with the rougher characters in the upper gallery. Noisy bantering passed into a moderate throwing of oranges, and moderate throwing into pitching and vulgarly vicious flinging.

There was a brief cessation of hostilities when four boys, dressed in clothes that had been discarded by courtiers as shabby, walked onto the stage with brass cressets and placed them in dark corners, lighting the candles. Then, in idle gaiety and great freedom of spirit, the confusion recommenced, the orange women calling and laughing shrilly and urging the gallants to further efforts in their fusillade. One fellow in a dirty red jacket and foreign-looking cap climbed down from the gallery, roaring something that set those who heard him bursting into laughter, but reaching the pit, he was met with so lively a reception that he was glad to retire, which he did by way of the king's unoccupied box.

Claude Duval, having no taste for the rough and tumble play, sat close in his seat near the stage. Then, as two or three orange women came in with fresh supplies, his attention was led to one, a slip of a girl of no more than fourteen summers, whose crying of her wares was more of a whisper than a call. Struck with her appearance, her pretty face and fine eyebrows and the nut brown shock of curling hair, and moved with a kind of sympathy, he bought her entire stock of fruit, not forgetting the basket, and handed his purchase to a woman older in the trade. At that the girl stared with eyes big and round with interest.

"You are new to this business," said Claude, and at that she laughed modestly enough and showed a row of gleaming teeth. Then bobbing a brief courtesy she made to leave.

"Mistress Knep," she explained, "will scold if I return not soon with the money."

"Heed not your Mistress Knep, whosoever she may be," said Claude. "Sit in this vacant seat by me and tell me your name, for you are too gentle a creature and too young to be selling oranges in all this coil."

"Nell Gwyn," answered the girl, and surveyed Claude with interest. Then she went on with vivacity, giving many little bird-like nods, and so told the page that her great wish was to sing, which being the case, she intended, she said, to be an orange girl and sell China oranges "until some lover of music discovers my gift and liking."

"A cruel and a foolish dream," said Claude gravely.

Then she chattered on, telling him of many things, of her home in Coal Lane, where it seemed, were often street fights and men were rough. Yet when she sang, especially an old song, "Summer is a-coming in," the noisiest gathered to listen. With glee she added that a lord once passing that way in his fine clothes had heard her and stood to listen. His name, he said, was Buckhurst, and her song being finished, he had told her that he would take her some day to Epsom Wells where great folk were, so that her fortune would be made.

Hearing that, Claude looked grave and said that he had no great liking for Lord Buckhurst, but the girl seemed not to hear, rattling on merrily, in vast delight at finding some one to listen. The talk was interrupted when a gayly dressed man with fat red face and thick lips, Buckhurst himself indeed, catching sight of the girl, bore down on her with a shout.

"The singing maid of Coal Lane," he called.

So there were hurried and confused greetings with Claude Duval unable to say a word good, bad or indifferent because of the rules of court procedure, and, before he well knew what was afoot, my Lord Buckhurst was on the stage saying something into the cloud of noise, and little Nell was standing by his side most demurely, her brown curls a frame for a rose-blushing face. When Buckhurst had finished talking he stepped to the side of the stage, where he was joined by his sallow-faced friend, Lord Sedley, and at once a fiddle struck up. Then Nelly, after making a pretty gesture to soften the noisy crowd, lifted up her head like a bird to sing, her silver voice pouring out over the cries and noise, stilling it to heavy silence, and she sang:

> "Here's a health unto his Majesty, with a fa, la, la,
> Conversion to his enemies, with a fa, la, la.
> And he that will not pledge his health,
> I wish him neither wit nor wealth,
> Nor yet a rope to hang himself."

There was a sweeping motion of the arms and hands, a kind of engaging, all-embracing gesture, and, like a fairy who had gathered all wills to hers, she encouraged and led the house in the chorus which came with a roar from stout lungs and many of them:

> "Nor yet a rope to hang himself,
> With a fa, la, la,
> And a fa, la, la, la, la."

So there were hurrahs so hearty and so intense that the strange girl wept and trembled with the effect she had produced. Buckhurst took a step forward, his hand outstretched, but Claude was quicker, and, regardless of custom and everything, offered his hand with a bow, as though she had been a court lady, and led her to the seat by his side, she smiling though pearls of tears were on her cheeks. At the same moment the duke and the king entered the royal place so that the huzzas that hailed the song mingled with those that greeted the king.

· · · · · · · ·

Now, the play was dull with long speeches and much poor wit, so the king yawned once or twice. But for little Nelly, seated by the side of Claude Duval, it was sufficiently glorious and she was all heart, all sympathy. There came a moment when she jumped in her seat like a pleased child, and it was at a happening that caused the king to applaud and made the other players look like weaklings and sluggards. For on the stage, dressed in red and white with a fluttering scarf of many hues, leaped a dancer, and she was lithe as a whip and graceful and light. Up and down the stage she went, never for a moment still, always at ease and full of gayety, winning her way into all hearts there with her smile. Soon she broke into song, still dancing, and, by the magic of her art the people saw, not an actress on the stage, but a sweet shepherdess in a magic garden. She sang a ballad, new to those there.

> "My lodging it is on the cold ground,
>   And very hard is my fare,
> But that which troubles me most is
>   The unkindness of my dear,

Yet still I cry, O turn, love,
   And I prythee love turn to me,
For thou art the man that I long for,
   And alack, what remedy!

I'll crown thee with a garland of straw then
   And marry thee with a rush ring,
My frozen hopes shall thaw then,
   And merrily we will sing.
O turn to me my dear, love,
   And prythee love turn to me,
For thou art the man that alone canst
   Procure my liberty.

But if thou wilt harden thy heart still,
   And be deaf to my pitiful moan,
Then I must endure the smart still,
   And tumble in straw alone.
Yet still I cry, O turn, love,
   And I prythee love turn to me,
For thou art the man that alone art
   The cause of my misery."

After that the show went flat, says a writer of the time. By some magic, Mary Davis, the dancer, won every one, from King Charles to lively Nelly Gwyn, and there was neither eye nor ear for any other. And because of the song and the singer there was a vacancy in the ranks of the court pages and that summer night, at high moonlight, Claude Duval as knight of the road bestrode one of the king's horses on Hounslow Heath, his back turned on the court forever, a reward on his head for his capture dead or alive. And the reason was, that of all men in England he alone had dared to tell his lord and master the truth.

. . . .

The interview had been short. After the play, the king sent for him, and, after a little boisterous laughing and the asking for the name of the pretty maid who sat next the page at the theater, the which Claude privately resented, Charles the king showed Claude a jeweled ring of great beauty of workmanship. "A pretty piece," said the monarch, flashing it and turning it in the light of a candle. "A man in Cologne wrought it and for Louis of France, I hear, but held it at not a penny less than seven hundred pounds."

The king looked at the jewel as a child would look at a new toy, his eyes shining with pleasure. Then he beckoned Claude to a niche, out of hearing of the two men-at-arms who had entered, and who stood in the doorway with young Selwyn commanding them.

"Duval," said the king, "it was a lucky thing indeed that you softened the heart of your old Midas and the turn shall not be forgotten. Another thing I would have you do to complete the work, for, certes, had you not brought us the gold, I could not have had this from the rascal of a jeweler at Cologne. As I said, music is better than gold, but he or she who hath both is happy indeed. So, that one may be happy, I would have you carry this ring to Mary Davis who at the theater sang about a rush ring. 'Tis a costly enough gift, but a king must be no niggard when sending gifts to a queen of song. So carry it to her, Claude, taking these two men-at-arms as your guard, and to-morrow thou shalt be dubbed 'Sir Knight.' "

The king had talked on, looking fondly at the ring, and seeing nothing of the fire of anger that flashed from Claude Duval's eyes, but a sudden movement on the part of the page caused the king to glance up, and he saw the young man strike a defiant attitude. A startled look shot across the monarch's face.

"Knighthood at the hands of a king whose feet are of clay!" retorted Duval, daring greatly in his burst of excitement and ire. "Such gold as I brought, I fought for, little thinking that it would be laid at the feet of a dancing girl."

At once the king's wrath flooded him and his eyes went wickedly red.

"Treason, by heaven!" roared the king. "Blockhead you are!" He clapped his hands then, calling to Selwyn to arrest him. Claude sprang to one side in time to avoid Selwyn who came with drawn sword, the men-at-arms behind him; then, with two steps, he was at the window, and leaped out, landing lightly enough on the turf. He looked neither to right nor to left but sped across the lawn, leaped the privet hedge and made straight for the Mews. In the stable a horse stood saddled waiting for its rider, some one high in the court. Not many used stirrups of silver gilt. A gold piece thrown to the stable lad prevented delay, and a shaking of the rein was enough. Nor did Claude Duval slacken speed until he felt the soft earth of Hounslow Heath beneath his horse's hoofs.

—5—

Says the old ballad, of Claude Duval:

> When I was mounted on my steed,
> I thought myself a man indeed;
> With pistol cock'd and glittering sword,
> Stand and Deliver was the word
> Which makes me now lament to say,
> Pity the fall
> Of great Duval
>   Well a day,
>   Well a day.

A plumed hat had he and horse trappings of red leather, with silver bit and stirrups, and two diamonds shone like stars at his belt. At his side was a dagger with gilt-dressed leather case, his spurs were of gold and the scabbard of his sword showed neither speck nor stain. These were the things of the eye, but in his heart there were golden dreams of setting crooked things straight, of letting lowly folk go free and taking heavy toll of those whose worldly affairs were in happy state.

Many things that were strange he did, even to stopping rich men in London streets and at the palace gates, but none was stranger than the attack upon the king's wagon which carried money for the king's troops and from which he took three thousand pounds. For, within a few miles of St. Paul's, the wagon halted: at Staines it was, and in the courtyard of the White Hart Inn. And there, in the great oak-paneled room which was hung with bright pewter, a room pleasant enough with its open windows that gave upon an old walled garden shadowed by six old beech trees, the officer met a pleasant young man who sat at dinner. They struck up an acquaintance and dined together pleasantly enough on white bread and fowls roasted on a spit, and over the wine and walnuts there was talk of France and of Louis le Grand, and of the elegant young gentlemen about his court. From that, talk passed to Whitehall and King Charles, and the officer was vastly astonished to find that the young man had more than a passing acquaintance with great ones at court. Lightly enough he tossed off the names of lords and of ladies, spoke of duke this and earl that and sir the other, and, by the merest chance, dropped a remark which revealed an intimate acquaintance with the king himself. So, as he listened, minute by minute the officer grew more respectful, as needs must he who touches royalty at second hand. On his side, the officer, a grizzled fellow, disclosed that he had been in the service many years, had seen battle and had borne wounds with small reward in the past, and hope of none in the future. "Yet," said he, "though a dog's life, I like it, perhaps because I know no other."

He looked aslant at Claude as he said that, and it

was a look that told his hearer that he feared he had said too much. But Claude laughed heartily and called for another bottle of wine, saying that not one, but every true man, condemned the service as a bondage that held a man too strongly in the leash.

"A leash it is," said the officer, and sighed heavily. "Here I am at Staines with an old sweetheart at Longford, but a light ride off, and five times this year have I passed between Windsor and London without seeing her."

"*Nom de Dieu!*" laughed Claude Duval. "How soon would a thing such as that be mended did the king but know your plight. A word in his ear and the thing's done. Or, for the matter of that, without a word to him, seeing that others speak for him, think for him, act for him. So for a couple of hours, what difference? Am I not going the same way? And would I not aid an old soldier? Doubtless your men are honest, and if not—" He left the sentence unfinished and touched his sword.

"But the signed order—what of that?" asked the officer shaking his head mournfully.

"Tush!" said Claude Duval. "Have I not said that others act for him? If this was Whitehall, I would be writing the order myself in the name of the king. In the navy there is Master Pepys buying and selling and giving and ordering. Do you suppose the king knows of the rope here and the barrel of apples there? And, anyway, you will need no military absolution, for none need know. Go you to Longford, see your friend and meet me again at Egham where the wagon shall stop until you arrive. No one shall touch your gold. Or, if you are afraid of your own men, faith, I'll carry it on my saddle." He added by way of after-thought, "That, however, I would not care much to do, for such weight spoils good leather."

"Nor would I ask that," said the officer, "though it would be to my liking in a way inasmuch as I would know of its safety. Certainly, a luckless life has been mine with men deserting because of the pay being past due. So it is that I have kept a sharp eye open, a little fearing that my men would help themselves, their pay being late."

Claude made light of the man's doubts. "Go," said he, "and be of good cheer, but stay not too long lest I be tempted to walk off with the gold myself."

At that witticism the captain laughed merrily, then there was more talk, the advancing of objections for swift removal, and the upshot of it all was that Claude Duval agreed to do the old soldier a favor, taking charge of the wagon and men while the captain rode to Longford, and to that end all was arranged, so for Longford the soldier set out.

It was certainly in Claude Duval's mind to take the whole of the money for his use, mainly that with it he might be enabled to play the fine gentleman in France. Yet being open of hand as well as high of heart, there were times when the slightest of things changed him.

So, the train coming to a farmhouse, an old rambling place of red roofs and tall chimneys, many-gabled and rose-hung, the men were surprisingly greeted by a little group there with silence and glum looks. It was the more curious because at other places sunny-haired and blue-eyed children had stopped their play to see the sight of gaily-dressed commander and bronzed men-at-arms. Sometimes women had waved a hand, or men in the fields had lifted spade or rake or scythe by way of salute, and, in return, the soldiers had shouted something cheerily. Here, in a place fair enough to see, the man looked sourly and the woman's eyes were red, as though she had been crying, while the children showed neither interest nor joy. And all this in a place with garden bright with flowers, and fields vivid green against the pale hills beyond. So, though the wagon had creaked past the house a little way, Claude Duval turned bridle to say a word, bidding the men halt, which they did, believing him to be in command by order of their captain.

"What is wrong in this place?" asked Claude of the yeoman, and at the question the fellow hung his head and plucked his black beard, not answering for a few moments.

But the gates of talk being unlocked he told his tale, and it was an old one. The landowner, one well on in years, had married a young wife comely and lively, but her lord was a churl, stingy and sour. That was by way of introduction, the sorry tale being one of debt and the black-bearded man's inability to repay a loan made to his father who was dead. So on the morrow, the day the debt was due, the lord would arrive, and, there being no money in sight, man, wife and children must leave the place, though the bones of their forefathers were in the churchyard over the hill.

All of that the men-at-arms heard, for, seeing the talk going on, they had drawn within ear-shot. The wagoner was the first to speak, saying that he knew the tale to be a true one and that it was a crying shame. The lord who owned the land was a churl indeed, living not near his lands as a good man should, but nigh to St. Alban's and hard by the house of a certain Lord Bacon long since dead, but for whom his own grandfather served as gardener—that the wife was a sweet young thing from France, cherry-cheeked and fond of dancing—that the black-bearded man was as honest a fellow as the countryside held. There was much more of it, for the wagoner was long-winded and entangled himself in the telling of his tale, looping back often to take up forgotten threads.

"To-night," said the black-bearded man, "the lord will be at Rickmansworth Inn and to-morrow here, where a room must be prepared for him."

"And all these years we have spent here with naught but a bare living," put in the wife, a motherly kind of woman with clear gray-blue eyes.

"By all the saints!" said one of the soldiers, "it is all true and well I know it to be so, for my father and this man's father fought at Worcester together. Such a fellow as the lord can come to no right end, a man with gold and jewels and rich cloths and silver dishes in his house."

"Knowing the true state of affairs, a good king would soon mend it," put in another.

The third soldier growled at that, saying that in his opinion the king was too busy with his pleasures and mad humors to look into the affairs of his subjects, but him Claude Duval silenced with an uplifted finger shaken in warning.

"Not too rough with your tongue, my man," said he in a voice that was fairly soft and kind notwithstanding the words. "Mad humors the king may have, but it is because of one of those mad humors that I am here. So softly and fairly in your speech lest you do mischief with your tongue not meaning it. Now, to my thinking, it all falls out well enough for I am one of those sent by his majesty to minister to his subjects."

Having said that he pondered a while, then put questions to the black-bearded man like a lawyer. What was his debt? What other money did he owe? Had he flagged in his work? Did he attend to his duty at church? There was much more of it, soldiers and wagoner listening with deep interest. At the end, Claude said that it seemed as if the man came with clean hands, though the lord's were, in a manner of speaking, unwashed. "You may put aside your griefs, my man, for if you have been falsely and treacherously used, all will be mended when the king learns of your trouble."

"That may well be as you say," said the black beard, "yet kings and judges are not always swift in their righting of wrongs." Then he added, because in his heart he feared that by his talk he had upset his own apple cart. "By that I mean not that kings are dilatory, but that the affairs of state are so many that the king on his throne must be weary listening to tales of woe, so many there be, and we must bide our times; yet, in that biding, other things may go awry."

"I much fear that his majesty has talkative knaves in his land whose tongues wag too freely in criticism," said Claude Duval with seriousness. "Indeed, with such, I am at times minded to let things go their own way crookedly until they straighten themselves. That justice may be slow, the delicate balance dancing before it evens, the king well knows. Indeed, that wrong may be done none, there are, in the realm, men sent by the king to relieve distress, and on such a mission am I. But think not that the king's gold is to be flung away with careless hand."

At that speech there was a raising of eyebrows and a whispering, and at once, all about Claude Duval was an air of respect, the roughest there becoming placable in disposition.

"Said I not," said the black-bearded man to the wagoner, "that did the king but know of our plight, all would be well?" and the wagoner nodded many times and turned to Claude with what promised to be a long tale, but was stopped.

"Yet one gives not money as you scatter grass seed. How, think you, should his majesty render account to the lords and the commons?" That said Claude Duval. "No. By no means," he added. "To Egham we must go to do this business, where there is a clerk and a churchman to testify concerning the expenditure and your own good conduct, and to make out proper papers so that all may be as safe as the Tower of London."

The black-bearded man became very grave suddenly. "At the inn," he said, "I owe a little score, the which I forgot when I told of that which I owe."

"Nor knew I of that ale-house score," said the woman, and might have said more had she not been stopped with a gesture of warning by the wagoner. So she set her face like a mask, tightening her lips and lifting her chin.

So on to Egham they went, the black-bearded man walking behind the wagon and Claude Duval riding ahead, and presently came to the Duke of York Inn where they stopped, and traces were loosed and horses watered. A sturdy-looking fellow with a sun-browned face who sat on a bench gazing idly at the horse trough was sent to bring the clerk and the minister, which mission he did speedily.

The churchman was a little man of localized plumpness, full of sudden smiles and frowns, and, being made acquainted with the matter in hand, grew very busy and serious, saying that it was one of the greatest moments of his life. "And having done all properly, sir," he said to Claude, "my petition to you is that you make the king to know that the roof of the church is in sore need of repair so that on a rainy Sunday my very surplice is like a rag. Money, young sir, we sadly lack. *Hiatus valde deflendus,* you see. A sore lacking, much to be regretted." He added this latter by way of explanation to the soldiers as he waved a hand in the direction of the church steeple that stood against the violet sky.

"Rest assured, good man, the business in hand being done, it shall be seen that you are safely housed," Claude assured him, at which the good fellow wore a shining face and busied himself vastly with pen and ink and paper, watching Claude as a cat watches a bird, and finding hope and comfort in the whole transaction.

"It is no new thing to me, the doing of this," he told the little group of admiring parishioners who had gathered, standing at a respectful distance. Then, to Claude Duval he said, *"Consuetudo pro lege servatur,* which, your honor will say, is to the point."

The money bags were opened then, Claude Duval ceremoniously cutting the seals after calling upon the churchman to witness that all was in good order, and the gold coins were spilled in a glittering heap on a flat stone in the inn yard. First, five hundred coins were counted out to the black-bearded man, and he, in his great joy and relief from anxiety, called for ale for everybody. But Claude Duval frowned at that.

"Is that your way, sirrah?" he asked sternly. "Another like move and you return all and lose the good graces of the king's messenger." The fellow paled and shrank back, hearing that, and his wife, who had followed on foot, children with her, soon mended matters, taking the gold from her man with the aid of a stalwart soldier, and, face flushing red, assured Claude that there would be no danger of a single penny being spent on wine as long as she had two good hands to manage affairs. That business seemingly happily ended, Claude Duval bade the innkeeper serve all with good ale and see that the baker brought cakes.

"Fear not for the safety of the money, fair sir," said the churchman. "Well I know his good wife as the master of the house, nor being home will he gainsay her. She holds him in durance, and in the long run what Mistress Peer saith, Master Peer doth. *Ante tubam trepidat,* as one may say. Before the blast comes from the trumpet he trembles."

"Well enough," answered Claude. "Look well to it, for there may come on my heels those who would find fault with what I do. It is the way with the court. I ask but the good will of the king in the matter. Messengers come and go between Windsor and London and it would be ill for me were I found to have done something in error. True, his majesty would but smile, such being the love he bears me, but yet in that smile there might be bitterness."

As he spoke, Claude touched with his sword-point the heap of gold coin, thrusting the pieces this way and that until a pleasant sum was set aside. "That, good man, is for the roof of your church," he said, seeing which the minister so gaped with astonishment that Claude could scarce contain himself from laughing aloud. Indeed, to hide his merriment, he was forced to take a drink of wine which the landlord of the inn offered. While he drank, the churchman almost burst with his thanks.

"Thank not me but the king, whose messenger I am," said Claude. "Nor forget to drink a health unto his majesty."

For a time, after that, there was mad clatter with loud talking and much drinking with noisy appreciation: men were merry enough, showing their happiness with great explosions of laughter and, as men will, picking up their favorite children and lifting them shoulder-high to see over the heads of others, bidding them mark well the king's messenger and the glittering gold. Soon the cobbler, who was also a musician, brought forth his fiddle and struck up a merry air, on which a ragged Irish harper in old frayed coat and broken shoes who chanced to be tramping through the place, joined in cleverly. Lads took lasses then, leading them by the hand to a smooth, grassy place and soon there was dancing to the music, and one plump, high-colored woman who was the wife of the baker, outdancing them all, taking one of the soldiers by the arm and charging into the middle of the dance, making herself mistress of it at once. Nor was the clergyman any less inclined for pleasure than she, and, stripping off his coat in a sudden and wonderful burst of gaiety, he took the inn-keeper's wife, placing his arm about her suggestion of a waist and calling on all to follow. So the couple tripped their way to the dancers, followed by the little urchins of the village, and the merriment in the air was like that of a Mayday. An old rook in the top of an elm tree caw-cawed his delight and his fellows joined in so that the summer evening air was soon athrob with gladness and a kind of joyous noise seemed to come in fairy voices from the little hills as the echoes awoke. Nor were the animals slow to take part, for not only dogs and chickens, but early-coming cows, pigs, distant sheep and a gabbling flock of geese, led by a challenging gander, lifted their voices.

"Ill luck would follow me if I disturbed this happiness that the king's liberality has caused," said Claude Duval to the carter and the only soldier that stayed by the wagon. "For never would my master, the king, have his subjects stinted in their mirth. Yet it is high time that I set forth to meet a certain duke to whom I have to carry king's money, for dukes, like peasants, sometimes lack. So count me a thousand pounds into a bag and guard well the rest until the merriment is done. Then let each man and woman have a golden pound and each soldier five, not forgetting the carter, for it is the king's birthday. See to it, too, that the score is paid at the inn and look to hear from me later."

All that the soldier promised to do, a little amazed at the turn things had taken, but he was in no way suspicious of anything wrong, for he had stood sentinel about the royal palace and seen strange things done by courtiers and truffling gallants. And if there was an arrow of doubt in his mind, it would have been plucked out by the next words of Duval. "Do not fail to tell all this to the clerk, for the king's treasurer demands receipts in writing for all monies spent."

No sooner had Claude taken the reins of his horse, when a bonny-faced young girl with black hair and olive skin, who was standing by and a little in front of a curly-headed giant of a lad in earth-stained clothes, spoke. With many blushes she told her tale of how she and her swain were to be married, but, money being hard to get and the lord of the land a poor payer, the wedding had been sadly put off. Two of the king's golden coins, she said, would soon straighten matters, for she had been diligent with her needle and a good store of linen was in her chest.

Hearing the tale, Claude smiled, and it was easy for the girl to see that he had his heart set on giving the gold she asked. Yet he said, "No. No," and paused, to tease the maid. Then he went on, gayly enough, to say: "I have heard his majesty say that a king must be no niggard when giving gifts, and you belittle him in your asking. Not two, but fifty times two shall be your portion. So the soldier shall count out an hundred from the sack and—"

No chance had he to finish, for hearing that, the young girl danced for joy and clapped her hands, saying: "Oh, how good you are. Oh, how good is the king." As for the lad, he lost his shyness and called the glad tidings to the dancers so that they all came flocking, the coatless churchman in the midst of the throng, and there was talk in plenty about the generosity and the graciousness of the king and the goodness of his messenger and a very general blessing of the lucky day that brought the money to Egham. Then a leader of some kind in the place called out that the village should give a feast, and begged Claude Duval to grace it. But that he refused to do.

"Time fails me," he said, "for I have a bag of money to dispose of elsewhere and it would be shame for those who are happy to delay the happiness of others by so much as an hour."

He mounted then and started to ride away, but not alone, for along the village street, men, women and children ran by the side of his horse, cheering him loudly and thanking him. Boisterously enough in their joy they bore themselves, men slapping one another on the backs, and women waving, and arrived at the bridge, they sent him off with a parting cheer that startled the rooks to cawing louder than ever. So Claude drew his sword and gave a flourish by way of salute, then shook his rein and clattered down the road at a good round pace, all a-tingle with the sport he had made and well pleased with the day in which he had set a village wellnigh mad with joy.

—6—

More than fifteen miles Claude rode that evening, going past Longford, Drayton and Cowley, across low rolling hills, down a valley of tender green threaded by a silver stream, then, riding between two rows of thatched cottages, each with its glory of climbing rose bush and bank of sunflowers, he came at last to Uxbridge. There was brief stop there for the drinking of a glass of milk, then a riding into the meadow beyond, moist and green and refreshing to man and beast.

So he came to the moor below Rickmanworth as the sun was sinking below the Wycomb hills, and the glory of the sky was like the glory of a fire that did not burn, with bold crimson and gold and peacock green. Being wrapped in admiration of the sunset, he would have passed a coach on the moor had he not chanced to hear the harsh and high voice of a scolding man. Looking, then, he saw through the hole of the door a yellow-faced man, well wrinkled and with squint eyes, and by his side a sweet-faced, slight-built little lady, and at once the memory of the Lord of Egham flashed across his mind. Out came his sword then and, to the coachman, a sharp command.

"To the ground, man, and stand at the heads of your horses," he called, and the man, having no desire for trouble, scrambled from his seat so fast that his haste made Claude laugh. "Well done," he said. "A man so quick in action deserves good pay, and if your master is short in his giving, this will help." As he said that, he took some gold coins from his pocket and tossed them to the coachman.

But the old lord in the coach was by that time aware that something was afoot that should not be. He flung open the coach door and alighted, standing with one foot on the ground, the other on the step, a bristling old fellow. "What wouldst thou? What wouldst thou?" he cried, in a kind of snuffling voice, getting into the coach again when he saw Claude Duval masked and with drawn sword, a man tall and well shaped. But still he called, "What wouldst thou?"

"The thing that you hold most precious," answered the highwayman.

Hearing that, the old fellow fell into a great state of excitement, declaring that he had but little gold, with some silver plate the property of a neighbor, and he begged Claude to let him go in peace. Claude Duval stared, somewhat astonished at the man's craven conduct, and sheathed his sword, having no need for it with such a fellow. He dismounted and led his horse to the coach side. At that, the old lord leaped out of the other door and went running, waving his arms and shouting, "Thieves and robbers! Thieves and robbers!"

as though the furze bushes were king's men, and, having reached cover, he stopped, chattering and calling to the coachman, who paid him no heed, but stood grinning at his horses' heads.

There was one glance at the lady, whose face, in spite of the excitement, was bright and smiling, her cheeks like roses; then Claude whipped off his mask, took off his plumed hat and bowed low, and addressed her.

"Faith, it is the maid of honor of the Duchesse d'Orléans," he exclaimed in high delight.

"Ah!" said she, talking prettily with a French accent, "so this bold *voleur de grand chemin* is he who danced attendance in high-heeled shoes at Versailles. Let me see—his name, I remember, was Claude. Ah! Claude Duval. Yes. I have it. Claude Duval." She lifted a warning finger and continued, "He had no eyes then for any one but Diana in the *Plaisirs de l'Ile enchantée*. Well do I remember, now."

"You are unkind," said Claude. "We were to have danced a coranto, and you chose another partner."

"As ever when we met," she said winningly. "I am unkind, ungrateful, unjust. Long time will it take me to mend matters, seeing that I am the wife of—. Well, it matters little." There was a note of petulance in her voice and she shaded her eyes as she looked up, and their brilliance stood out the more. Then she said: "Well, Messire Duval, take your gold and stuff, and begone," and indicated some wallets that lay on the floor.

"Sweet lady," said the highwayman, "there are things better than gold."

"And what?"

"The keeping of a promise," he answered. "There was your promise made in the green gardens of Marly, the promise that we should step a coranto on that day that you were clad in a gown of russet and gold, the brightest one there."

She broke into kind laughter, and standing, gave him her hand and he helped her to alight, then went on his knee.

"Gold and jewels are to be won everywhere," said he, "but not the friendship of so gracious a lady."

"Have you clean forgotten my husband?" she asked.

"Would that I could," was his reply, and did not fail to notice her mock anger at the words. "Yet pardon me for a brief moment the while I pay my respects to him," he added.

Leading his horse to the clump where stood the old lord who had found some fancied shelter behind a solitary elder bush, Claude said:

"Sir, I crave your help and hospitality in a little business."

At once the old man fell to chattering about his gold, asking if ten pounds would not buy his way clear, but Claude paid small attention. Indeed, he laughed in the fellow's face.

"Keep your ill-gotten gold and welcome, every jot of it," said Duval. "This is a matter of a promise.

For your lady and I knew one another long before this, and once in France she granted me the favor of a dance fairly asked. That promise I would have redeemed here and now. So, you being a mannerly man as I trust, will you serve me as one cavalier should another, watching my horse the while we dance?" And, without another word, he thrust the bridle in the old man's hand very deftly and strode off to the lady, smiles all over his face.

At the edge of a smooth grassy place was a fallen tree, and the highwayman threw over it his cloak to form a seat, and to it led the lady. Then he took his flageolet and played the music of a coranto, a ravishing sweet melody, she, the while he played, smiling and nodding her head merrily.

"That was the tune," said Claude. "Master Humphrey made it, and at Marly you said it was beautiful. So I cherished it ever."

Then he offered his hand and she took it and rose, and while Claude sang the air he had played, the lady joining her voice with his presently, they danced in the sheen twixt sunset and moonrise, and to the servant who held the horses it was a wonder and a delight, though to the old man it was neither. The dance being finished, Claude Duval thanked her kindly and led her to the coach, saying, "And now the bargain is complete, there is one thing more." He went to the old man and took his horse again and led it to the coach side, the lord following in amaze. Nor did the old fellow's looks wander far from the gleam of the diamonds on Claude's belt or the glitter of his silver scabbard.

To the lady Claude said: "I have been too much out of gates lately to buy toys, yet I beg you to take the gift I offer, sweet lady of the green garden of Marly." As he spoke he tipped the saddle bags which he had taken from his horse, in such way that a ringing shower of gold coins fell on the seat beside the lady. "And this, too," he said, taking off his belt. "For therein are two diamonds, the which I have kept to remind me of your bright eyes, but having seen them again I can never forget them, wherefore the jewels to me are useless."

"Now the weight of the matter is all on your side," said she, and, leaning forward from her seat as Claude stood at the coach door, she kissed him on the cheek.

"Now God a-mercy!" said the old man.

Therewith, Claude Duval leaped to his saddle and so they parted, but for some time thereafter the lady said nothing to her lord, but wept quietly, although she was happy at heart.

—7—

The tale of that, and of many other like adventures did not die for the lack of telling, for Duval robbed much and stinted none and gold won was gold given. So when the day came on which he lay in Newgate, to the prison came

> " . . . ladies from all parts,
> To offer up close prisoners their hearts,
> Which he received as tribute due—
>
> . . . . . .
>
> Never did bold knight, to relieve
> Distressed dames, such dreadful feats achieve,
> As feeble damsels for his sake,
> Would have been proud to undertake,
> And, bravely ambitious to redeem
> The world's loss and their own,
> Strove who should have the honor to lay down,
> And change a life with him."

Thus sang the poet Butler.

And, indeed, to the prison went ladies from all quarters of London, ladies young and old, each paying her guinea for admission to the warder, each anxious to see and to talk with the young man, bright-faced and debonair in spite of his plight. So the flame of admiration burned wide and free and it was hardly without discomfiture that any one in the fashionable world declared that respects had not been paid to Claude Duval, while those counted themselves lucky who could tell tales of having been robbed by the knight of the road. Praise for him was everywhere—praise for his generosity, for his chivalry, for his graces. Then when the day came, the twenty-first day of January in the year sixteen hundred and seventy, Claude Duval, dressed like a prince in silk and silver, stepped into the cart at Newgate door and all along the road to Tyburn ladies in dark gowns wept at windows and men from the pavements saluted him, bowing as to a king. But at the scaffold he stood smiling, a flower in his mouth, his plumed hat in his hand, and when the hangman seemed slow, he scolded him for his awkwardness as one scolds a careless servant, stamping his foot as if to break the boards.

That night there was a lying in state in the great oak-paneled room in the Tangier Tavern and eight tall wax tapers burned and the bier was guarded by eight gentlemen in long black cloaks, who carried swords. From Covent Garden Church to the Tangier Tavern in St. Giles were torch-bearers, and, as those who carried the body marched, the flambeaux fell in behind, two by two and in quiet order. Near the church the air throbbed with the sound of muffled drums. So the procession passed and from streets and alleys and houses there swept into the train ladies in their coaches, countrymen, butcher boys, bakers, crossing sweepers and men and women from Covent Garden market. Some shouted and many wept, for when sentimentality is added to crime the crime seems lessened. And that was the end of Claude Duval, court page and highwayman, who died at the age of twenty-seven years.

A NET OF LOOSE FISH

*"The good old rule, the simple plan,
That they should take who have the power,
That they should keep who can."*

A NET OF LOOSE FISH

SEE in your mind's eye a procession of bad men. It is like a scene that resembles a pageant on the stage. There are all sorts and conditions of men—fellows flaunting in finery and double-dealing rascals tricked out as heroes. Blueskin, black-browed and athletic; Jonathan Wild, squint-eyed, squat, malevolent; Sixteen-String Jack, marching with happy swagger, ablaze with fluttering ribbons and laced hat and tasseled boots, with a crowd of admiring urchins following, tripping over themselves as they go, their eyes on their sorry hero; Jack Cade, wild-eyed and hasty, insolent of demeanor, heading a rag-tag and bob-tail, cudgel-bearing prentice lads about him; Robin Hood and his men in Lincoln green, all impudent and sun-tanned, each with bow at his back and quiver at his side; Simnel, the baker's son; Demetrius the False; the Unknown, who claimed to be the Prince of Modena, a diamond glittering runnion. Then a crowd of fellows who died or rotted in prisons, without a name—footpads, alley thieves, cutpurses, loafers, sneaks, hangers-on and, walking alone, Cartouche, robber without courtesy or generosity. But there are banners and bands of music, and a roaring song, and the Duke of Guise comes with music and his army of three thousand five hundred outlaws in coats of Spanish leather with sleeves of velvet, their breeches of scarlet cloth trimmed with gold, each with his leather girdle, from which dangles a cutlass full three fingers broad and two feet long; and so come those who rob on land or on sea, Kidd, Morgan, Bonnet, Gramont, Van Horn, Scowling Mowlbar, the Caitiff Pintes, Wild Conrad with his black flag and swarthy followers carrying firelocks and blunderbusses.

Then a wild mob, doers of violence in the name of a cause—blood-thirsty fiends and merciless boors with torch and sword, ax and hammer, mask and gown—sparing neither the weak nor the aged nor the helpless—mobsmen, torturers, cullions, riff-raff from watersides and human rat holes and secret chambers. With strange howlings and ululations runs a party of thugs, each man with seven red spots on his face and sinister cord about his waist; then the giant Gilderoy, six feet ten in his bare feet, with kilt and sporran and dirk, murder and lust in his eye, bending horseshoes and bars of iron as though they were mere twigs; men on foot and men on horse; Dick Turpin on his Black Bess, Swift Nick on that dappled mare which he loved better than his own flesh and blood, Juan Moreira, the gaucho of the Chaco, astride of Diablo, *lazo* and *boledores* neatly

HIGHWAYMEN

coiled, glittering façon thrust through scarlet sash; bearded men of the gold fields; swift desert riders, their accoutrements a-jingle with silver bells; wild horse thieves of the Andes; Jerry Abershaw, the lad who might have been captain of men, blazing into wrathful suspicion at a look; Jesse James and the Younger brothers; Black Jack and Tracey the outlaw; Ned Kelley, the iron-clad Australian bushranger, with clumsy headpiece of riveted iron and bullet-defying breastplate; a few women, Moll Cutpurse, Mary Read and Annie Bonnie: William Parsons, heir to a baronetcy, proud in his suit of white with blue facings, navy officer, Maryland convict and highwayman; handsome James Maclean, clever with sword or with pistol or with fist, a Jekyll-Hyde combination of gentleman and rascal, free-handed with gold and silver and banknotes; then a motley crowd—shabby heroes, glittering rascals, swindling inn-keepers, half-hearted scoundrels, shuffling fellows, swashbucklers, knaves most paltry and treacherous, scurvy and venal, rascals gay and debonair—here an ignoramus and there a scholar—Jack Sheppard side by side with Eugene Aram, Vidocq touching elbows with Earl Ferrers, Jerry Sneak arm-in-arm with Colonel Thomas Blood, slippery knaves walking with men of some candor. A rare show indeed, with gibbets here and gibbets there; fellows brave with drink carrying horse pistols, flourishing rapiers, hiding daggers; much bluster and tumult, much blood, much frenzy.

JAMES MACLEAN

FELLOWS of some candor, I said, thinking of James Maclean, soldier of fortune, who fought when fighting was to be done. For, when the last of the fighting kings stood at the head of his army on the field of Dettingen, Maclean was there; and again, when Prince Charles Edward took Edinburgh, there was James Maclean strutting about the Grassmarket in kilts, playing Cock o' the Walk on the bagpipes. At least all that has been said. The docket is not very clear. However, war being over for him, he could not turn to hodman's work. There was a visit to Amsterdam, which coincided with the great diamond robbery when the jeweler Nykerk lost certain precious stones, part of the Austrian regalia, then Mr. Maclean turned up in London town, seeking adventure as a kind of serious play. For instance, chancing to drop into George Taylor's gymnasium with a few friends, he heard a loud-mouthed gipsy fellow named Boswell proclaim himself as the master of boxing and the best man in all England. So Maclean stripped to the waist, entered the ring and, in short time, proved Gipsy Boswell's boast to be hollow.

Now, in those days, Philip Dormer, fourth Lord Chesterfield, sometimes walked the streets, and when he did so, his favorite way was down Curzon Street and along Piccadilly until he came to St. James's Street. At other times, instead of following Piccadilly, he would cross the park, pass Buckingham Palace, and arrive at St. James's Street by way of Marlborough House. But whichsoever way he walked, his journey ended at number fourteen St. James's Street, where lived Mr. Maclean, obviously something of an hidalgo, else he would not have made his home in the most fashionable part of town where kings and princes moved, and lords congregated. My Lord Chesterfield found James Maclean to be an attractive character, a gentleman in every respect, very active and fond of entertaining, to whose house came, sooner or later, every notability and eminent stranger. It was there that Theodore, King of Corsica, sat for a time in state under a canopy, a silver dish at his feet to hold such coin as his visitors chose to donate to help him regain his kingdom, though, to be sure, he failed to get enough to keep him out of the Fleet debtor's prison.

Nor did Maclean confine himself to the fashionable, for there was one memorable party at which Edward Wortley Montague, son of Lady Mary, was the guest of honor, and the young man who had been fisherman, chimney sweep, traveling showman, day laborer, abbot and Lutheran preacher, told the assembled guests why he had embraced Mohammedanism, as he sat like a

Turk, cross-legged on the floor, and chewed opium while the others drank wine. There was another day on which others gathered to enjoy the hospitality of Mr. Maclean, and the atmosphere was different. For James Newbery, the apple-faced man who printed books for children, was there, and also many bookmen and writers, notably the little prim bookseller Richardson, who had written Pamela, and the magnetic Johnson who stumbled about, clumsily, knocking little things down, and who entertained the company with talk of his days of hunger and hardship with the poet Savage.

Chesterfield found something exciting about Mr. Maclean's originality in whipping his company off on unexpected expeditions and unlooked-for places of entertainment—to Vauxhall, for instance, or to Ranelagh, or for water excursions in the river Thames with fiddlers in the boat playing Handel's water music. Often the party ended at White's, where there was high play, Maclean staking as much as any one and losing with good grace. Once, indeed, he dropped at a single play some twenty-one thousand pounds to my Lord Stavordale. To watch a man losing money with perfect nonchalance, making no sign of discomfiture, was fascinating to the polite lord.

"To see a man," said he to Horace Walpole one day, "with an absolute command of his temper, serene enough not to let any one discover anything by a display of emotion, is most excellent. Our friend, James Maclean, has the essentials for statesmanship."

"But," objected Horace Walpole, "his love for gaming is a sad vice."

"Ah! That may well be," said the other, "but the charming thing is that he gratifies his vice with delicacy and with secrecy."

"Secrecy in statesmanship may be thought desirable," said Walpole, "but it brings absurdities into political laws and institutions. I would like your Mr. Maclean better were he not so secret and if, from his conduct, something of his worse side might be inferred."

For Horace Walpole, like the rest of the bon ton, wondered at times what gold mine supplied the weighty wants of James Maclean; for not only did he keep a well-appointed house with a staff of capable servants, not only did he entertain lavishly and play deep, but he was singularly unlucky at cards, and, in addition, generous to an amazing degree. As for ill luck at play, the elegant Maclean laughed at that when friends said consoling things.

"Fortune is a whimsy jade," he laughed. "She gives to take away. Consider the case of my Lord Beachy last week. Fortune smiled on him and I dropped five thousand at hazard. The same night he won more than two thousand from the Earl of Ramsay. What then? On his way home his coach is stopped by highwaymen —masked rascals—this side of Edgeware, and not only does he lose his seven thousand, but his rings and watch and all else. I would rather choose to lose to a friend, giving him pleasure, than win to carry my gains to some scoundrel who claps a pistol to your head on Hounslow Heath."

As for his generosity, there was a dinner that he gave once, a men's dinner, well served and sumptuous. Some prominent people were there; a statesman and one in the foreign service; David Garrick, the actor, who attended in full court suit, embroidered with gold, in which he played his Macbeth; Sir Horace Mann, the friend of Walpole; the luckless Earl Ferrers who was so soon after to be hanged in a rope of silk for the murder of his steward; a couple of French gentlemen and Mr. Maclean's friend, Doctor Plunkett. At the table, talk fell on the new book, Joseph Andrews, and there was much laughter at Fielding's story of Joseph in the coach. From that, talk veered to highwaymen and then to diamonds, at which one and another passed about rings and jeweled snuff boxes for examination, admiration and comparison. Then a little dispute sprang up about the Sancy diamond, and from that the Koh-i-noor came to be talked about, and Maclean described it as he had seen it in India.

"But," said Maclean, "we make too great a fuss of diamonds. I know a place in Madagascar where they are common as stones in the London streets and may be had for the picking up."

So saying, he took from a sideboard a little box and carried it to the table. Then, "Look at this," he said, and sent spinning down the table a great ruby which he took from the box. To do something unexpected and extraordinary was quite characteristic of Maclean, so, while minds might have been busy, nothing was said, and the stone was passed from hand to hand.

It had not gone the round of the table when the host took from the box a gold cross set with wonderful stones of red and blue and green. The thing was a blaze of beauty, a toy of magic light under the candles.

Earl Ferrers picked it up and held it between his thumb and finger, calling on all to admire it. "Never," said he, "saw I a thing to compare with this for value and workmanship." He seemed to be unable to let it go.

"If you admire it, please to keep it," said Maclean smilingly. "A trip to Madagascar and such stones may be had by the handful."

Of course, in politeness, Ferrers refused the gift, but his host insisted, urging him to take it, making light of its value, and at last Ferrers complied, full of hearty thanks.

Then from the box came other things—amethysts, sapphires, diamonds, rubies, pearls, opals; stones cut and uncut, stones polished and in the rough, until the table was dotted with glittering things and the treasure box was empty. Nor was there guest who had not a jewel pressed upon him as souvenir. Maclean laughed a little at their profuse thanks, saying that he was, as he supposed, lucky. That being the case, what better could he ask than that his friends would share his good fortune?

"And," he added, "since there are a few stones left, I beg of you to take those that please you. Plunkett, you take the ruby. It will look well if set in the head of that walking cane you carry. And you, Ferrers, take the blue diamond, which is of finest water." So, every one being loaded with gifts, the dinner ended.

Then, in one of his sudden bursts, Maclean proposed a boat party. He had, he said, a new barge on the river and good men to row it, and they could go to Chelsea. So all walked across the park, except Garrick, who had theater matters that called him; and they came to the broad stairs that led down to the lapping waters at Westminster and there embarked. Servants piled away hampers of eatables and bottles of wine, and a man with a French horn played heartily.

To gain the help of the incoming tide, the rowers pushed to the middle of the river and there, by chance, ran into a light evening mist. It was just thick enough to hide both banks of the river but not thick enough to muffle sounds, and presently their ears caught the noise of swift oars striking rowlocks in a way that betokened the coming of a boat at a rapid pace. Soon there slid out of the gray fog, and towards them, a light boat, manned by two men, each with a pair of oars. There was a man at the helm and another, half-standing, at the bow. The latter had a beardless face and he was dressed in a white coat with blue facings and knee breeches. Seeing the other boat, there was a moment's silence, but the chattering and the music broke out again until it became clear that the boat was headed directly for the barge and that there was danger of collision.

"Head your boat off! Head your boat off a little!" called Maclean, but the words had no effect, for there was no change in the boat's course. Instead, the rowers pulled faster and the man in the bows stood up. Then, those in the barge saw that he was of small frame and well dressed, so they supposed him a passenger until they saw him put on a black mask and take in his hand a pistol. At the same moment the steersman also masked himself. So well the rowers pulled that it was clear that they had designs, and soon those designs were evident, for by skillful handling they brought their boat alongside the barge, and a moment or two saw them with the two rowers holding fast to the gunnel of the barge, the oarsmen on both barge and boat having taken their oars inboard to avoid smashing. Then up jumped the steersman and pointed his pistol while the white-clad man in the bows jumped aboard the barge, his pistol cocked.

"Into the river with your swords!" he commanded. "The first to make a move is a dead man!"

"A pretty pass indeed—" began Dr. Plunkett as he stood up and half-drew his sword. At the words, the steersman of the little boat presented his pistol to the amazed doctor's head and the sentence was left unsaid.

"These are my guests and it is a piece of foolishness and an uncivil business," called Maclean. Then, as by an afterthought, he said to his friends in the barge,

"But we are caught on the hip and must have no dead men." "You are right," said Dr. Plunkett, and threw his sword over the side at once. With something very like a groan of physical pain, Ferrers followed suit, seeing which, the others made no move to resist.

"Every one will place into the hat all his valuables or risk his life," said the masked man in white. One of the rowers then stepped into the barge and, going about among the guests of Maclean, held a hat under the nose of each in turn. The first was one of the Frenchmen, who emptied his pockets, and, having done so, cursed the robber, saying, "May the rope of Judas himself hang you." Then, having thus relieved himself, he sat down and glowered. Out came watches, money, rings, snuff boxes, trinkets and the precious stones so lately given as mementoes, and all being well stripped, the river robbers climbed back into their boat and disappeared with their booty in the direction of Westminster, untouched and unpursued.

As might be expected, the trip to Chelsea was abandoned then and the party sought the shore, Maclean lamenting the sore trouble to which he had unwittingly put his guests.

. . . .

At 14 St. James's Street, Mr. Maclean, and Dr. Plunkett who accompanied him, found a visitor in the little garden behind the house. His was a short, narrow-built figure with sloping shoulders, and he looked the smaller on account of his white clothes, while his

"Into the river with your swords," he commanded

wide and low forehead and weak chin made his head seem too heavy for his body. Maclean greeted him happily, saying:

"Ha! Parsons, so we did the job well, eh?"

"Why, yes," answered the man in white. "Much depends on the manner of attack. You saw my way. I always strike terror into their hearts first thing. Seeing me in the bow of the boat with my pistol, not one in your barge would have dared to move. They were outwitted at the first moment. Had you not been there I would have managed it." There was an air of immense pride and conceit about him as he talked, strutting up and down the little gravel walk. "You see," he went on, after a pause, "costume counts, too. These white clothes of mine set my figure off well."

Maclean showed his teeth in a big grin. "It stands to reason, Parsons. It stands to reason. Dinna think, laddie, we don' appreciate all that. Yet, mayhap, my plannin' had not a little to do with it all."

"Something, yes, to be sure," agreed Parsons, talking very quickly. Then he became suave and leaned forward, touching Maclean on the knee. "But never forget my attack and my habit of striking terror into the hearts of those I meet. Never forget that. Why, when I was in Maryland, I made some bold moves, I assure you. Not an Indian in the country but feared me. Had the governor but listened to me, had he not been jealous, I would have driven the French from the Ohio valley. I had the name of being the boldest in the country, and a wild country it is, and full of wild men. But fear and I were always strangers. Why, when I was a boy at Eton school, the very masters modified their manners and addressed me with a 'yes, sir,' and a 'no, sir,' and a 'by your leave, sir,' for they mightily feared my bodily strength. So also it was at Jamaica. Single-handed I faced a mob of revolting slaves. Give me show of sword and pistol and I fear no man. Stand me afore a mob and—"

"You'll stand before a mob at Tyburn, my man, some day, an you're not less handy with the bottle," said Maclean grimly.

Doctor Plunkett, who had not said a word, interrupted then. He had been sitting with closed eyes, although, in the moonlight, the braggart Parsons had supposed him to be listening with studied civility.

"Suppose you set out the booty," said Plunkett, and exchanged looks with Maclean. "We had to keep our eyes on our own diamonds and stones lest some of our guests forgot when you collected from them."

"Well, without that it was a good haul," said Parsons. "With the stones and the gold and the watches and the rings, it reminded me of the time I stopped my father's own sister in Norfolk. Did I ever tell you about that?"

"We will hear, but we may as well get the business done first," said Maclean, and, as he spoke, he lifted and set close to where Parsons stood, a garden table.

Then Parsons began feeling in his pockets and producing things, telling them as he set them on the table. "Seven watches, and some rings. And here is gold. Some eighty-five pounds. Then there is silver which I have not counted but—"

"Heed not the siller," said Maclean. "We'll lay aside the stones which are mine, and share the rest."

"Two gold chains," went on Parsons. "This one I took from Ferrers. And here we set aside the stones, two from every man, which calls to mind the time I was in the army and—"

"Never heed the army," said Maclean, and pushed back to the center of the table the pile of treasure.

"Well, that's all," said Parsons. "And now let us see a bottle."

"Was there no ruby?" asked Maclean, looking into the foliage of a great tree that grew in the corner.

"Had there been, I would surely have remembered it," answered Parsons. "No. There was no ruby."

"But the ruby I myself gave you," put in Dr. Plunkett.

"There was no ruby," insisted Parsons.

"Then there must have been some mistake," said Maclean, carelessly. "But what of a jeweled cross that Ferrers handed you?"

Parsons at once donned the robe of the martyr.

"What would you accuse me of?" he asked with a whine. "Think you I'd be false to my friends? Gadzooks! for less I'd have run my own father through.

Once in Maryland I killed an officer for less." Then there was a jeremiad. He had, he said, planned and risked his life. He had contrived and played his part well. And all for what? To be suspected. To be accused. To be brought to this. And after Maclean had had the easiest end, and Plunkett, on his part, had done almost nothing. So he, the son of a baronet, had been made a cat's paw. Or were they joking with him? Surely they were. Then his overwrought self broke down and he whimpered for a time like a whipped boy. A half-minute of that and there was another change and he stood up, threw out his little chest and denounced them as unworthy. He demeaned himself with them. He would have no more of their company and would leave the house then and there. And he took a step or two away.

"But not so fast. Not so fast," said Plunkett.

"I done my best and you accuse me," whined Parsons. "Me, the son of a baronet and once an officer in His Majesty's Royal Navy, and afterwards in the army."

"Yes. Yes. 'Tis a cold world, and, doubtless, we are all hopeless scoundrels," said Maclean. "Nevertheless, I doubt not but that you have made a mistake, being no clerk, and 'tis best that all should be right."

"But I was insulted. You called me a thief," cried Parsons.

"And the name fits like a glove," retorted Maclean.

"So come, Parsons, out with the jewels and of the real booty take your third share and ha' done with it all." He turned his back on him.

"Look out, Maclean!" called Dr. Plunkett, as Parsons drew his sword.

"Come on. Come on," snarled Parsons, making passes in the air.

"You infernal fool," roared Maclean, swinging round, and swore savagely as Parsons made a lunge at him. Then Maclean struck out with his left hand and caught Parsons on the shoulder with such force as to send him reeling. The sword fell at the feet of the Scot and he picked it up and broke it across his knee. Seeing that, Parsons drew his pistol, but, at the same instant, Maclean's great fist tightened on the back of his neck like a vice and the pistol was dropped. Then there was a change and Parsons found himself being thrashed with a riding whip, lashed across the shoulders and the back, and, from under Maclean's arm, he could see Dr. Plunkett shaking with laughter, intensely amused. Being at last released, Parsons flung himself on the grass, weeping, talking incoherently, threatening things, thoroughly frightened.

"Come. Have you had enough?" asked Maclean.

Parsons had, and said so with many tears. It had all been a mistake. Maclean and Plunkett had been too rash, had been too serious to take a piece of merriment, for it was but a joke that he had intended. Certainly, there had been a ruby, and if they had but waited a little he would have surprised them. For safety's sake he had placed it in the toe of his shoe. And, sure enough, the shoe being taken off, there it was found. As for the jewelled cross, it was in the lining of his hat, placed there so that no common thief might get it, had he been attacked. They owed him thanks for his care and forethought.

Maclean made mighty chuckling noises. "Some jokes are too practical," he said. "So practical that they hur-rt. And the fact is, Parsons, for the son of a baronet, you carried the joke a leetle too far. Sensible men modify their jokes, I think."

So the stuff that was working capital was set aside and the booty shared. Although Master Parsons suggested the opening of a bottle, his request went unheeded and he was urged firmly to the garden gate. As a result of the joke, there was a coolness, a gulf not to be easily bridged, and a promising partnership in crime was dissolved.

. . . .

It was the sheerest of accidents that led to the abandonment of the house at number 14 St. James's Street. Everything in the adventure had been planned with elaborate care and all went well up to a certain point, then came the finger of fate.

About three o'clock in the afternoon of a day in November, in the year 1749, Mr. Maclean stepped into the street dressed in the height of fashion, and walked slowly along Pall Mall. His man servant followed at a little distance, leading a horse, a splendid animal.

Outside Taylor's coffee-house, Mr. Maclean chanced to meet David Hume, friend of many years, with whom was a bright-eyed and eager young gentleman whose name, Hume said, was Edmund Burke. So, at the invitation of the hospitable Maclean, they turned into the coffee-house and over their chocolate they talked, while the servant remained outside with his master's horse.

Half an hour later Mr. Maclean appeared, mounted his horse and rode westward, bowing and saluting this acquaintance and that, halting here and there to talk with a friend, until he reached Hyde Park. There he met Dr. Plunkett, who was also mounted, and together they cantered, two highly respectable gentlemen taking the air. But afternoons are short in London in November and twice around the park brought them into moonrise. Then they sought the shadow of the trees and waited.

Soon there were the sounds of hoofs and of wheels, and Dr. Plunkett said:

"It must be he, for two would hardly be coming this way now, and if he left Holland House promptly, he would be about here by now."

Both men slipped on black masks, and, as the coach came in sight, Dr. Plunkett put spurs to his horse and attacked the out-rider with such suddenness that the lad fell to the ground and had much ado to keep clear of the startled horses. Maclean rode to the side of the coach, cocked his pistol and thrust it into the coach through the window.

"What stupidity! What stupidity!" called Mr. Horace Walpole, the occupant of the coach, when something happened of which the precise details are wanting. At any rate, by some mischance, Maclean's pistol went off and the highwayman's heart fell as he saw the genial gentleman, who had sat at his table, fall to the floor of the coach, while a trickle of blood laced his cheek. Without delay, bridles were turned then and the two robbers sped away.

"I was attacked," wrote Mr. Walpole to Sir Horace Mann, "by two highwaymen in Hyde Park, and the pistol of one of them, going off accidently, razed the skin under my eye, left some marks of shot on my face and stunned me. The ball went through the top of the chariot, and, if I had sat an inch nearer the left side, must have gone through my head."

The tale was told by the post boy, who recognized the horse Maclean rode, and next morning the news was known all over town, those who could, going post-haste to No. 14 St. James's Street, but the accomplished gentleman-highwayman had left for safer fields. Nor was there news of his whereabouts, although at White's, two days later, Mr. Templeman received a letter signed by James Maclean, which said:

". . . *The accident, my dear sir, was both singular and unfortunate, and linked my name with Mr. Walpole's in a strange and regrettable way. . . . Under the circumstances, it would be unwise on my part to appear in town, for there are not wanting those whose rage and malice might place me in an unfortunate position.*"

. . . .

Unhappily for Mr. Maclean, his absence from town did not quiet the rage and malice of the town, and, though he confined his operations to the suburbs, there was one fine day, three months later, when he was recognized in New Palace Yard, where was gathered a crowd to watch the hangman publicly burn a book entitled Constitutional Queries, directed against the Duke of Cumberland. That was on January 25th, 1750. He was not seen again until June 26th of the same year, when he attacked my Lord Eglinton's coach on Hounslow Heath. But, then, lurking in a dry ditch near-by was a poacher who fired his fowling piece, and the horse that Maclean rode was brought down. Other men chancing to pass that way, the gentleman-highwayman was laid by the heels, and in time tried, convicted and met his fate like a gentleman. Nor would it seem that among his many accomplishments, Mr. James Maclean was entirely uninvested with the gift of prophecy, for, on the day of his condemnation, he told the judge that he had always feared that Newgate would be his end.

But in his seclusion, many who had tasted his hospitality and many who had not, called to see him. "Lord Mountford," wrote Horace Walpole to Sir Horace Mann, "at the head of half White's coffee-house, went to look at him in Newgate, and on Sunday three thousand people went to see him and he fainted away twice with the heat of his cell."

JONATHAN WILD

FROM that writhing mass of odd fish, of sinful things dredged from the depths, we gingerly lift one, particularly loathsome —a thing of tentacles and malevolent eye, a blood-sucking, loathsome creature, a parasite that throve on parasites. For Jonathan Wild was the foul being that fostered crime, hatched crime, commercialized crime. Born in a year of corruption when London's very air seemed foul and festering, the year when the great plague raged, he grew in the midst of moral corruption and became a center of social corruption. Like a presiding genius he watched over the world of crime, urging innocents into lives of thievery, highway robbery, housebreaking, pocket-picking, murder, shop-sneaking, double-crossing, thuggery. Sixty years he lived, becoming a very Hercules of crime. His was the organizing mind, the mind that controlled, the mind that suggested new ways to evade the law. Authority he wielded and the base of that authority was fear. Did one of his victims refuse to execute some new crime, then over him hung the threat of the gallows. A word from the thief-taker and the gates of Newgate yawned. Cortes destroyed the ships which might have offered means of retreat from Mexico, and Jonathan Wild destroyed all roads by means of which his victims might hope to pass to better ways. A glance from the thief-taker and the boldest winced. Wild hung the gibbets of all England with the chained bodies of his victims. Whoso disobeyed his orders, fell. To rule over an invisible kingdom, binding innocent and guilty alike with the chain of fear, was his dream.

The way Jonathan Wild gained his power was thus: He had been but an indifferent kind of lad, fond of attending public executions and pillory punishments, disinclined for honest labor and willing to turn a penny when it could be done easily. So, there being some who considered it great sport to pelt those who sat on their coffin in the hangman's cart, or who stood bound head and hands in the pillory, young Jonathan discovered an opening by the sale of dead rats, cats, dogs and ancient eggs, and, while the pay was not great, the raw material was to be had for the picking up. Occasionally, a careless citizen was inattentive to his watch-chain or purse, and some there were who left their walking canes at the doors of taverns and of inns, and therein lay further chances for easy enrichment, which young Jonathan was not slow to see. At the age of

HIGHWAYMEN 199

eighteen or so, young Wild was a gawky kind of lad, no comely youth as to face or complexion, for his eyes were wide set apart and there was, an historian says, no hollow between eyebrow and eyelid. Because of his ill looks, he was prevented from following the profession for which he yearned, that is, being a man servant in the houses of the wealthy so that he might be able to locate the family plate and jewels. So he lived in semi-seclusion in the neighborhood of the Old Bailey until the year 1684, when a daily post was opened between London and Epsom. Then it was that there was fine utilization of opportunity, for many went to Epsom to drink the waters and so there grew up very soon a considerable pleasure place. An assembly room and gaming house were built, there was a ring as in Hyde Park, there were daily horse races, dancing, cudgel-playing and wrestling and to the Wells went pleasure-seekers in hackney coaches. While all this went on, highwaymen and pickpockets were busy and, bringing their gains to London, found some difficulty in disposing of the booty at a reasonable price. Then to Jonathan Wild came the luminous idea, and he started a new life as buyer of stolen goods. But the young man was all for conservation of energy. There were easier ways of disposing of the things he had bought for little than by selling them again in the open market. That would mean a profit of a mere one or two hundred per cent on the original investment. Greater gain was easily possible. So, taking a trip to the Wells, he made it known that he possessed a particular aptitude for locating missing property. He was a sort of pre-incarnation of Sherlock Holmes, as it were, and, given description and suitable recompense for his trouble, would trace missing and stolen things. Should the lost article have a mere sentimental value, the happier he would be, he announced, to discover it. There was quick response. Many, many things had been stolen—jewels, watches, purses from high and from low, and those who had lost were willing to pay for the restoration of the things. Back to London then went Jonathan Wild, turned over the stock in his cellar and, not without making a tale of the immense difficulty he had encountered, handed to the original owner for a heavy price that which he had bought at a trifle.

From so small a beginning great things grew. The house near the Old Bailey developed into an office, and Jonathan Wild, shrewdly alert to opportunity, advertised himself as Restorer of Missing Property.

But there were thieves and highwaymen who patronized other similar but less famous establishments, and the brilliant scheme of Wild involved monopoly. Soon then there was a new and effective combination, a kind of by-product, for Wild, learning of this man and that who patronized the opposition, threatened dire things should his establishment be consistently ignored. On the other hand, having persuaded some one in authority to stimulate the forces of retribution by the offering of rewards for the capture of thieves, Wild became thief-taker, delivering to justice those who were not his customers, and, before long, walked the streets with a silver wand of office. With him there was no cold standard of moderation. Thieves traded with him or were hanged. Those who had been robbed, either traded with him or were robbed again. Individual achievement on the part of any robber was rewarded. Slacking met its deserts with prompt arrest and imprisonment, for some crime perhaps forgotten of men, but not by Wild.

Soon there was a classification and a tabulation of knowledge. Such and such a coach would be here or there on such a day, and this wealthy man or that would ride. So highwaymen in the Wild entourage were ordered to attack and the system of planning and dispatching grew until there was high efficiency and all England came under the paw of the Master Thief-Taker, manager of the Office for the Restoration of Missing Property. As a well-appointed railroad company has its departments for the maintenance of way, the maintenance of equipment, traffic, transportation and civil engineering, so Wild's organization had its divisions and subdivisions, for Jonathan had the organization point of view. So there were lines of varied activity, men were fitted to tasks, these for stealing from churches, these to operate at fairs, others to commit burglary, to ride the highway, to steal from children bent on errands. In the basement beneath the Office for the Restoration of Missing Property there were mechanics, handy men who could change the appearance of a watch or a chain or a brooch; others who obliterated the monograms on gold and silver plate; others who clipped gold and silver coin; forgers; counterfeiters.

He met the disturbing factor of a glutted market with masterly ease. At seaport towns he hired warehouses wherein was stored the booty not easily disposed of, and, his barns waxing fat, he bought a ship, appointed an agent in Holland and exported on a large scale.

Sometimes there were complaints from headquarters that the thief-taker was not sending enough criminals to the bar of justice, and then disciplinary power was wielded and those who were not diligent and had brought too little to the master, were sent to prison. So it was that Blueskin, highwayman and friend of Jack Sheppard, was sent to Newgate.

Blueskin, however, had known the hunger and darkness of a prison cell before, and resented the dull drudgery of life under the thumb of Jonathan Wild. In the court of justice with Wild evidence in chief against him, Blueskin put a firm face on the matter, roaring out to the judge his tale of Wild's perfidy. "Your thief-taker is a thief-maker," he cried, but that the court would not believe. Wild, stepping from the witness box, held a whispered consultation with the judge and soon after the judgment was ordered read.

"Prisoner at the bar," read the clerk, "you shall be

taken to the prison from whence you came, and put into a mean room, stopped from the light; and you shall there be laid on the ground, without any litter, straw, or other covering, and without any garment. You shall lie upon your back; your head shall be covered; and your feet shall be bare. One of your arms shall be drawn to one side of the room, and the other arm to the other side; and your legs shall be served in like manner. Then, there shall be laid upon your body as much iron, or stone, as you can bear, and more. And the first day, you shall have three morsels of barley bread, without any drink; and the second day you shall be allowed to drink as much as you can, at three times, of the water that is next to the prison door, except running water, without any bread. And this shall be your diet till you die."

"Such courts of law I will die fighting," shouted Blueskin, and, leaping out of the prisoner's dock, he snatched a sword from a guard, bounded across the floor and made a pass at Jonathan Wild, cutting his throat severely. Indeed, had it not been for the thick neck cloth that he wore, Tyburn would not have had its due on that early summer day in the year 1725. As it was, the thief-taker fell to the ground screaming, the court officials gathered about him, and, in the confusion, Blueskin reached the street.

. . . .

One day, six weeks later, Mr. Wild made an attempt to take matters into his own hands in a way that was altogether too manifest. It was at The Gold Cup, an ale-house within sound of Bow Bells that the affair took place, and The Gold Cup had a disreputable flavor as a flash case. Too many men had been traced there, and from that point all sight was lost of them. Again, it was too popular with many who had no visible means of support. The landlord, when questioned, pointed to the fact that the great thief-taker, Jonathan Wild, was there often and had found nothing wrong. However, on this particular day Mr. Wild and a party of five sat at a table drinking, not in plain sight of common folk, but in a rear room, and to that rear room there went, running, a shock-headed boy, who shouted:

"Harry Stamps is a-comin' and it's hempen fortune. He's grabbed. He's grabbed."

"Some cowen's blew on him," said a fellow with a black patch over his eye. "I knew it. I knew it when I see the beaks go by."

"Stow your gab," shouted Jonathan Wild, and went to the door to see, close to the inn, a little crowd of horsemen and, tied hand and foot on a led horse, Harry Stamps, the eagle-faced captain of the highwaymen who operated on the Kentish road.

Wild pushed to the middle of the road, his five companions and the inn-keeper following and called on the officer in charge to halt.

"Make way! Make way!" said the officer. "We have accounts to settle, you and I, but this is my prisoner." He turned his head slowly to his men, then looked at Wild.

"I'll make you sing small, my fine fellow. I'm thief-taker, I would have you know," cried Wild.

"Thief-maker, as Blueskin said," retorted the officer, and at the sally his soldiers laughed. "But out of the way, fellow," he said brusquely, and pushed against Wild with his horse. Then Wild grew furious and yelled for help, laying hold of the bridle of the officer's horse and tugging at it wildly so that the horse, in its pain, reared. A black-bearded man bearing a crowbar ran forward then, holding the heavy steel above his head with both hands and thrusting as though to drive it in the officer's back, but a soldier, seeing the move, brought down his sword on the fellow's head and he fell, the bar ringing sharply on the cobblestones, and the hoof of the horse missed him by an inch. On Wild's face anger gave place to terror, and he ran back to the inn door where a little crowd had gathered. From the inn-keeper he took a pistol and fired at the officer and the ball passed through the fleshy part of his shoulder. In another moment there was a fighting crowd and the little band of soldiers with their prisoner became a target for a volley of stones, of broken bottles, of things flung from upper windows, and fifty hands tore at the prisoner to release him. Hearing the noise of the fighting, others came, bearing cudgels, hammers, anything picked up at random; elbowing one another, thrusting weaklings forward; fellows in rags, loud-mouthed and foul; the spewings of alleys and of underground dens. Once or twice there were shots and one man ran screaming, holding his jaw with a blood-stained hand. So thick soon became the press, that the soldiers and their officer, white-faced with pain from his wound, were like tossed things in a sea. Nor did they hesitate when it became a case of swords, though they struck at heads and backs with the flat of them. At the rear there was a grim struggle, and a noisy, howling mob succeeded in taking the trapped highwayman, Harry Stamps, from his horse; the fellow was prone on the stones, a dozen hands tugging at his ropes to loose him.

"Look!" said a soldier to the captain, and pointed with his sword to a crowd of some thirty coming from the west and at their head a horseman, a tall figure in a coat of flaming red. "Blueskin, it is. He who escaped."

In a voice like a trumpet, the coming rider shouted: "Down with Wild! Take him, men!" and swung into a rapid trot. A shout that was like an explosion came from the men who followed. Afterwards there came a rushing confusion and Blueskin and the soldiers were like men cutting weeds for a time, and the packing people fought without order or plan, but there was tremendous screaming, much shouting. Then it became known that some had retreated within the inn and that the door of The Golden Cup was being shut, though with vast difficulty because of the press of people who sought entry. Down to the ground leaped Blueskin, and, like a battering ram, he flung himself into the mass, striking, beating, tearing furiously. His plan no one knew, but in very few moments he had fought his way into the inn and behind him flowed a crowd.

In the street was a confusion like that of disturbed ants and the sore-pressed soldiers had recovered their prisoner and were fastening him in his place. Who was who none could tell. Those who came with Blueskin had mingled with those who had stood with Wild, and fighting had ceased for the most part, though there were minor skirmishes and warfares that had degenerated to mere scufflings. Suddenly a boy shouted "Look!" and at once all eyes were turned upwards to see, at an upper window, Blueskin wrestling furiously with Jonathan Wild, the thief-taker. At first they were seen behind the window, but there was a fierce lurch and both men fell against the casement which went crashing to the street. The fighters turning, those in the street saw that Wild had a knife in his hand, but Blueskin's hand went inch by inch, advancing slowly, crawling up the other's arm, to elbow, to forearm, to wrist, until it seemed as though things had come to an end, and the men must stand there locked together until others released them. But Blueskin had sinews of tempered steel and those who looked saw a spasm of pain cross Wild's face as his wrist was strangely turned, and the knife fell. A wriggle and a swift unclasping and clasping, and Blueskin had the burly figure of the thief-taker in his arms and was forcing him out of the window while Wild screamed and tore at the hands that held him. No one saw what followed, for there was a vision of something descending, a spot of scarlet in mid-air, a sense of something seen clinging, then every one was running and crowding to see the two figures that had fallen to the stones. Blueskin was the first to get to his feet, and no sooner had he done so than he jerked Jonathan Wild up savagely and stood glaring furiously, his nostrils dilated.

"Your prisoner, sir!" he said to the officer, and, at a sign and a word, Wild's hands were tied and he was roped to run by a soldier's saddle.

"Blueskin! Take Blueskin!" yelled the thief-taker. The old fox snarled as he said this.

"Silence! Forward!" commanded the officer, swaying a little with the pain of his wound, and the little troop moved on, followed only by one or two adventurous spirits, and that night Jonathan Wild slept in Newgate.

• • • • • • • •

Mysteriously the word was passed that the king of crime had fallen and by twos and threes, within the space of an hour, some three hundred people were crowding before the house in the Old Bailey neighborhood. There was little but idle staring until the tall, athletic figure of Blueskin was seen pounding at the door of the house, then the crowd which had been loose, jammed close—so close that Blueskin was crowded against the door, unable to move. From some one in the crowd came the cry of "Break down the door," and from hand to hand, over the heads of the crowd, was passed a sledge hammer.

"Stand back!" roared Blueskin, and the crowd pressed back, and those near enough saw the young giant dealing terrific blows on the stout oak. But a lad saw another and easier way and clambered up the wall, stepping from projection to projection until he reached an upper window which was unbarred. That he shattered and entered, and soon had the oaken door open. The crowd rushing in came near to crushing him against the wall. Two minutes later, every window in the house was flung open and men were from attic to cellar. Four troopers in the street called on the mob to desist, but the order was greeted with yells of defiance. Inside there was looting. The collection of years was there—money, gold and silver plate, jewels, church vessels, watches, articles of furniture and embroidered silks, weapons, housebreaking tools, the coiled ropes that had hung his victims, and instruments of torture, fetters, knives, bottles of poison, a pillory complete, masks, gibbet chains. With laughter and execrations, things were thrown out of windows to be scrambled for by the crowd, and those who found treasure were set upon and robbed, the robbers again being robbed. Soon there appeared carts in the streets and these were loaded down with odd things taken from the house—doors and casements and iron railings pulled from the front until the building stood a gutted thing, black and empty. Fire did what hands left undone, and it was not until a mounted body of troopers appeared that quiet was restored.

And on the fatal day, hoots, yells and execrations greeted the burly fellow who sat on his coffin in the death cart. It was a people gone mad, a people filled with the blood lust, that lined the streets between Newgate and Tyburn, for of all odd fish, Wild was oddest.

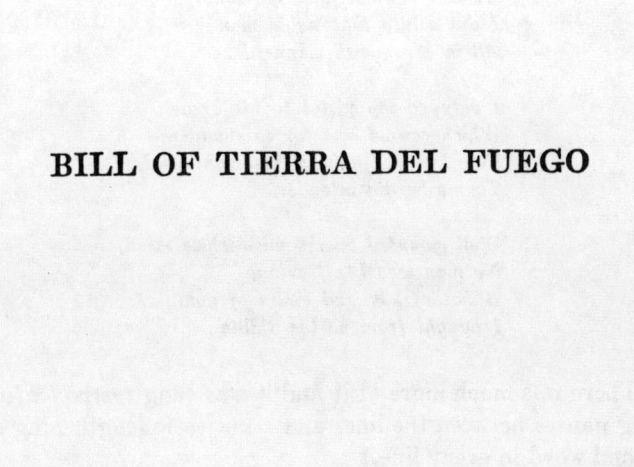

BILL OF TIERRA DEL FUEGO

(As we sat in camp, we would often sing, tunelessly, perhaps, but nevertheless heartily. Bill Downer's only song was this:

> The first great man that e'er I robbed,
> He wor a great lord of honnor,
> I did salute that noble man
> All in a rogueish manner.
>
> I clapped my pistol to his breast,
> Which caused him for to shudder—
> Five hundred guineas in bright gold,
> To me he did intender.
>
> Well mounted on my milk white steed,
> No man was I a fearing,
> A hat of silk and spurs of gold,
> I bought from mister Shilling.

There was much more of it and it was sung *tempo lento*, with long pauses between the lines and a majestic lengthening of the second word in every line.)

BILL OF TIERRA DEL FUEGO

—1—

BILL DOWNER and I rode hundreds of miles together—from Punta Arenas to Chuput, from Chuput to Deseado and from Deseado to Gallegos. Together we loaded wool in Santa Cruz, we sheared sheep in the Falklands and, on a venture that now looks to me most insane, we sailed in a cutter from Monte Dinero to Port Stanley and would have gone across the Atlantic to South Africa had we not heard of a gold strike in Tierra del Fuego. So I knew Downer very well indeed, and, doubtless, many who have sailed the seven seas and know the Magellan country will find his name by no means new and, be it said, his record somewhat cloudy.

Cloudy because he became a kind of highwayman, and the most extraordinary thing in the whole story is the dovetailing of events whereby he passed easily from honest man to rogue. His transition astonished me the more because I knew him as a man full of life and anxious for happenings, but the core of his philosophy was resignation. "A man," he used to say, "ought to prove himself by the suffering he can bear. Thoroughbreds don't yelp." But, when the test came, so small a thing as the loss of a pipe threw him off his balance. Neither was it his pipe, but our pipe, a community pipe, a pipe common to three of us.

It came about this way. When Downer and I heard of the gold strike in Tierra del (we always knocked off the "Fuego" in talking of the place down there) he and I sought out Axel the Dane, sold what we had of sealskins, horses, and odd impedimenta, and bought a so-called whaleboat. Then, one fine day, after a celebration in Punta Arenas, we started for Bahia Inutil, a desolate coast on the west side of Tierra del Fuego, avoided alike by sane men and ships. For three months we had rain, hail and sleet, for three months we suffered from cold and wet and hard fare, for three months there were dismal things, but the troubles of each day were swiftly forgotten when the campfire blazed and the coffee was scalding and sweet, and when we smoked as

Axel played the accordion. But during that three months, one way or another, we managed to lose our pipes, and then came a campfire gloom. Without smoking there were no yarns, no fantastic lies, no songs, no castle-building, no planning of wonderful trips in the future. Even the accordion was untouched and lay under Axel's bunk, and we fell into the dumps and moped.

But Bill Downer mended matters. For, prowling about the beach one day, he chanced to find part of a teapot, one of those million things cast overboard by some steward's boy to be washed ashore after many adventures. It was, or had been, a common earthenware affair, brown glazed and brittle, the kind often found handleless in establishments not well appointed. Seeing possibilities, Downer carried it to the tent and chipped, hour after hour, until at last he broke the spout loose and made of it something that did fair duty as a pipe when a small stone was dropped into the bulbous end by way of a tobacco stopper. It was awkward to handle and the mouthpiece was uncomfortably large. Indeed, for satisfactory service the thing had to be held at a certain angle so that the man smoking it looked like a conch-blowing Triton. Still, it's any port in a storm, and the thing served at a pinch, and after a day's hard digging, with the improvised pipe going, there was a tremendous sense of comfort in the camp, especially when a hail-storm raged and the air outside was bitterly cold.

About nine one morning when Bill was smoking, it being his turn, the pipe was shattered, and the fellow was so distressed as to be almost inconsolable.

The mischief was caused by Ropper, a fellow who had a concession from the government, at least he said so, permitting him to mine all the gold in Argentine Tierra del. Certainly, it may have been that Ropper's men were invading—Bill held that they were—and it may have been that we were in fault, for we had been following a creek on little expeditions and it is quite possible that we had crossed the boundary line out of Chile. At any rate, the mischief was done, Bill, as I have said, smoking as he handled the big five-pronged fork pitching the washed gravel out of the boxes; Axel the Dane shoveling in the manto; I knee-deep in water at the tailings. One moment we were thus, then there came a shout from the hill-top and Bill wheeled about in surprise, and, as ill luck had it, the shot that followed the shout shattered the precious pipe and Bill grew profoundly anguished. There were confused happenings, and, without a word other than objurgatory, Bill dashed up the declivity, fork in hand, intent on charging the men in ambush. Seeing that he was taking a responsibility with big possibilities, we followed with revolvers.

There was neither bloodshed nor fighting. At the top, we saw that our attackers had already gone. Mounted on fleet little Patagonian horses, they had reached the ridge a half-mile away while we climbed the river bank, so all that we could do was to gesture and promise terrible things should they ever again cross our paths. Then we assumed various attitudes expressive of philosophic unconcern.

When we got back to the river we saw our folly, for it was speedily evident that there had been two attacking parties, and, while the one had drawn us off on that silly, fruitless chase, the other had smashed and splintered our boxes. The camp, too, had been rifled and our gold taken, though everything else was left untouched. So pregnant things were said to the unsympathetic hills, and we denounced Tierra del as a place unfitted for civilized man.

We fretted considerably, and that night, over tin pannikins of scalding black coffee, Downer sounded a warning to the universe. Thenceforth and forever he would be no planless man. He would have a mission, and the mission would be to drive all monopolists from the land. He would be revenged upon Ropper and Ropper's men. He would be a Jesse James, a Juan Moreira, a Robin Hood, and he would league the Ooan Indians into a destroying band and drive white men from the island. There was a diminuendo presently, though he talked and rumbled and grumbled far into the night and, with great deliberation, sketched out a life of freedom for himself as a sort of fantastic extremist, until, his anger passing into sullenness, he sat for hours, fist supporting chin, staring into the fire. Looking at him as he sat, the dancing firelight painting his face, he brought to my mind some old Viking instead of a modern Nova Scotian who had left seafaring for a land life. But certainly, in spite of his philosophy, he had not borne suffering with equanimity, and instead of the breaking of the pipe being regarded as a mere incident, it was magnified. Out of his rage came a most tremendous reality.

—2—

The incident broke up our expedition after a little ineffectual remonstrance on my part. We sailed north, hugging the coast, and so came to Porvenir, a land-encircled gulf because of the tortuous strait; a blue, oval mirror framed in green with an edging of silver where tiny, lapping wavelets touched yellow sands. The settlement itself was a group of some seven little houses snuggled in a warm fold of wooded hills, the largest house being both inn and saloon kept by one known as the Greek. With plenty to eat and to drink and with unlimited tobacco, Bill Downer's depression vanished as if by magic, but his determination to live the free life remained unshaken. There was a spirit of allegory in him, and he said:

"Sheep wouldn't be handled by a man if they didn't flock. Me, I'll flock alone from now on."

So when the three-masted schooner, the *Martha Gale,*

From end to end of the boat he went, striking, cursing, threatening
(*See page 236*)

dropped anchor, we went aboard, and, after a little parley, sold our whale boat and shared the proceeds. Axel and I took passage for Patagonia, but Bill, true to his determination, stayed in Tierra del. From the Greek he bought a dark bay horse, reputed to possess exceptional qualities and great powers of endurance, and, as we shook hands at parting, he spoke with authoritative assurance of his future career.

I recall that the captain's daughter, whom I worshipped, looked with interest at Bill as we dropped past Venablo Point on the tide. She spoke to me in French, asking me what he intended to do there in that grey land, and I had to search diligently to find the right word.

"*Voleur de grand chemin,*" I hazarded at last, at which she looked puzzled and wondered prettily where were the Great Ways in that desolate place and what there was to steal; and so did I. Still, a highwayman he was, though a knight of the road without gay trappings and silver gilt, and instead of gorgeous suit and laced hat there was a red-flannel-lined coat of leather, a broad-brimmed hat and long spurred boots. Behind his saddle was a stout bull-hide lasso neatly coiled, and, handy to his reach, a set of business-like boledores so disposed that he could loose them in an instant and at a touch. A tightly rolled guanaco capa formed his bedding and light saddle bags held handy, necessary things.

— 3 —

Before long there were robberies in the neighborhood of Sebastian Bay, headquarters of the concession, the miniature kingdom ruled by Ropper. For instance, there was the famous raid of one, when Bill, having found his way into the enclosure on a dark night, alone and single-handed took the amalgamated plates from the gold-washing machines and cast them into the sea. There were confused accounts of his escape, of his being discovered while at work and of his finishing his job under fire, of his dash up the beach and swift running from cover to cover, of men doing things without plans and running and dodging and falling headlong, of Bill finally gaining the outer edge of the settlement and firing at haphazard. It was a silly, a grotesque business and no one was seriously hurt—one or two suffered from flesh wounds and one man broke an arm, stumbling over an excited dog. The raid, it appeared, commenced a little after midnight and the excitement lasted for less than an hour, so, in very short while, windows were again darkened and watchmen slept. But that same night Bill made a second attack, riding into the settlement with his horse's hoofs muffled, and making straight for the company store. The awakened watchman stared at the outlaw with half-fascinated terror, then decided to parley. For a moment, he said, he meditated making an alarm, but his fears overruled him.

Downer's tale, told long afterward, was that the fellow aided him very materially, leading the way to a back door and, not only disclosing the place where the revolver cartridges were kept, but carrying and placing box after box in the saddle bags. Then, with greatest amicability, outlaw and watchman sat down to a little lunch on canned sardines, Palmer's biscuits, and Crosse and Blackwell's marmalade, and at the close, the watchman found a bottle of Martell's three-star cognac. On leaving, the watchman stipulated that Bill should bind and lightly gag him and, to the end that he might not be uncomfortably long in durance, should see to it that an alarm was given as he rode away. All of which was done.

Another time the horses belonging to the San Sebastian Bay outfit were driven off, the whole *tropilla* of thirty. For some time thereafter horses bearing the —SS— brand were found here and there at widely separated points; three at Ushuaia on the Beagle Channel and four in possession of a gold-digger at Punta Marina, two in Gente Grande and three at Porvenir. In each case the owners had "papers" to show that they were innocent purchasers.

Then one day Ropper was out hunting and met Downer face to face. The Argentine was riding his favorite mare, a creature with the legs of a gazelle and the body of a race horse, fleet and beautiful. Throughout the land the lustrous Agna was known, for no creature was more splendid. Silver trappings and cunningly wrought hide work had she, and Ropper rode as easily and beautifully as Cunninghame Graham.

From his place high on a hill at the intersection of two valleys, Downer watched the horseman far below, going at a good round gallop through the sea of grass. In the clear summer air of an early December he could see as plainly as though he looked through a field glass, and his heart leaped with a kind of joy as he noted horse and rider, the dancing mane, the flying tail. A good horse and a good ship never failed to lift the heart of the man. The perfection of form in them ravished him, filled him with a strange warmth of happiness. For a while he contemplated the rider as he went from violet hill shade to splash of sunlit grass, then he turned the head of his own horse and commenced the descent of the steep hill, making for the other valley because it would be easy to force a meeting with Ropper at the point where both valleys met. And the meeting fell out precisely as Downer planned. Reaching the valley, he was hidden from Ropper by the foothill, so waited until he heard the thud of unshod hoofs, when he pressed knees to his horse, took the rivulet at a leap and crossed his victim's path before there was suspicion.

"Stand!" called Bill in a hard and ferocious voice.

Then queer things happened. For the briefest moment there was hesitation; then Ropper, making no effort to resist, threw his hands high and, in a manner possible only to an expert horseman, flung himself out of the saddle and landed lightly, his hands still upraised. The long gaucho reins fell on both sides of the mare which, after a little snort of surprise, wandered off some dozen yards and fell to grazing. That left the highwayman pointing his revolver at a man on foot, at which he was filled with a sense of vexation. Slowly he lowered his weapon and, with his left hand, rubbed his eye and mumbled imprecations.

Ropper spoke with a smile, carefully feeling for words in a language not familiar, and so softly and casually that he seemed to be talking to himself.

"You are Be-el the robbaier. Eh?"

"'S me," admitted Bill, taken aback at the turn things had taken.

"And, as I learn, you are, what is the word, salteador de caminos, a road rider?" At that Ropper deliberately dropped his hands and said, by way of explanation: "It is a *boberia* to stand thus, and I have no weapons as you see."

Bill reined his horse close to Ropper and placed his hand on his shoulder with an air of physical compulsion. "You got to hand over what I want, hombre," said he.

"*Comano*," agreed Ropper, looking frankly at his assailant. "But a man hunting carries but little. A rifle, my watch and chain, this ring—it is all. You may have it."

"Them's nothing," put in Bill with a deprecatory gesture. Then he shot a glance at the mare and nodded. "That's what I'm after," he added.

For the first time in the interview there was a trace of emotion on Ropper's face and he moved, instinctively, in the direction of the mare. "By no means," he said. "The gear, perhaps, but not the animal, mastaire Be-el."

A certain perplexity filled the robber then. "I was," he told me afterwards, "flabbergasted. There was the fellow making no sign of fight, and me in the saddle with a loaded revolver cuttin' up. I felt silly." He began to say something to Ropper, but was stopped with an uplifted hand. The educated man, quiet and well-mannered, puzzled the would-be robber.

"You see, mistaire Be-el, I find the incident amusing. But it is not amusing when you ask for my horse. To give the valuables is nothing. But the mare I have trained. . . . Certainly, no!" It was the air of finality about Ropper that perplexed Bill. Somehow, he felt that he could not overcome the determination in the man's eyes.

"But the mare—" Bill recommenced and was again interrupted.

"My man," said Ropper, throwing open an argumentative hand, "I am perhaps in a way reech, but I care for the fun and not for the gold. I am no wealth lovaire, but I am a horse lovaire and my liking for Agna—" he halted for a satisfactory expression, then said: "Ah! What shall I say? It burns within me as the sun burns in the sky."

Bill rubbed his nose in vexation. "It's the mare I'm

after," he said. "You just got to hand her over. I don't want to be mean, to do mean things."

It was clear that things had gone past the shooting stage and into the talking, and Bill dismounted as a visible sign of his unwillingness to take unfair advantage. His horse wandered over to the grazing mare, and, after a little sniffing and rubbing of noses and soft whinneying, the animals fell to munching grass together. For a moment Bill meditated a dash at the mare, a leap into the saddle and flight. Then, before he was well aware of how things were turning, there were civilities, with Ropper offering him a cigarette, and, after that, the production of a silver pocket flask and the pouring of a little benedictine, golden as sunlight. In that friendly drinking was "the hell of it," to use Bill's expression. For, by all the rules of South American hospitality, Chilean, Peruvian or Banda Oriental, it is impossible to drink with a man and then rob him of his dearest possession. So talk set in and there was frankness of discussion on the points of well-known horses, and soon they were interested to the point of forgetfulness of surroundings. At one moment there was a keen glitter of appreciation in the eyes of Ropper when he heard Bill declare that he wanted to belong to himself and to be beholden to no man. That was when Ropper offered the highwayman a position as horse buyer. The strange upshot of it all was that after a couple of hours there was a shaking of hands, and, in spite of Bill's refusal, Ropper pressed on him his diamond ring and a fancy worked cabresto which the highwayman greatly admired. Moreover, they rode together, and, as evidence of courtesy, Ropper exchanged mounts with Bill for three miles or so and, when they came to a smooth stretch, Ropper proposed a race. So reins were loosed and riders bent low, and horses, their hearts on fire, broke into swiftness, and Bill won on Ropper's mare. So there was hearty laughter and warm handshaking as they parted, Ropper telling the highwayman that he would not have missed the meeting for anything in the world.

"For all that," answered Bill, talking over his shoulder, "I'm not goin' to let up. This here island's got to be free for any one to come an' go, an' there ain't no law."

"Except the law of might," added Ropper.

—4—

Bill Downer's exciting moment came when the *Vellarino,* Argentine transport, was fast on a sand bank in Bahia Inutil and waiting for high tide to float her off. For, having a shipment of gold dust to send to Buenos Ayres, the major domo at San Sebastian decided to send the gold across country under guard, to the end that many weary miles of steering through the crooked Magellan straits and a looping down southwards might be avoided when the steamer was afloat again. So from the settlement went the little caravan, in charge of an officer who carried many medals on his breast. He had in his band three brown, lithe men from San Julian and a dilapidated young man from Liverpool, England, fugitive from his own country as well as from Chile, and the treasure was in a leather sack strapped across the saddle of a pack horse.

The highwayman chose the Santa Maria valley for his battleground, and, being out of cartridges at the time, had a feverish experience. From the shelter of a bush on the western bank of the river, a steep incline some sixty feet high, he watched the little cavalcade descend on the opposite side, watched them as they forded, watering their horses meanwhile, watched them commence the ascent, and then he had to depend on his ears.

The first man to appear was easy to manage, for it was the officer, a poor rider very heavily cloaked, who, having the best horse, was well ahead of his companions. Him, Downer allowed to climb out of the valley and ride a few paces. Then there was a whizzing in the air and the highwayman's lasso fell about the rider. His startled horse gave a leap and the rider struck the earth with a thump that knocked the breath out of his body. So Bill took his cabresto of soft hide and, in very short time, had him tied hand and foot. Being no very valiant man, he was a silent spectator of some of what followed.

With a grunt, the tightly cinched pack horse clambered out of the valley and then Downer did things swiftly. He pushed out and stood at the head of the path, his boledores a-swing. The first man was farther behind the pack horse than he had guessed, but well in advance of the three men from San Julian. It was the Liverpool lad, who, seeing the whirling balls, capitulated quickly.

" 'Ere. None o' that for me," he cried, throwing up his elbow to shield his face. Then he slid from his horse and went running down the slope, scrambling through bushes with vast alacrity. Seeing that, the Argentine men knew that something was amiss and the foremost one gave a shout and spurred his horse so that it went up the narrow path at redoubled speed. When his face appeared, the boledores were swung rapidly. There were three complete circlings and Bill let fly, the weapon whirling through the air true to its mark, flying low. The joint of the thongs caught the knees of the horse and as the thin hide wound and tangled, the hampered animal reared high to fall sideways, and man and beast crashed into a jungle of bushes to plunge down a declivity that was like a precipice. But both man and beast, tough and wiry, suffered nothing but a few bruises, and at the river brink the man applied himself to repair the slight damage.

Of the two remaining horsemen, the foremost dismounted and drew his long, keen knife with its eighteen inch blade. "El bandido Bee-el," Downer heard him say, and the other drew his revolver and fired, but at random. A second shot followed. Then Downer took his lasso, swung, cast, and missed. Down he crouched then, close to the edge of the declivity until his eyes were on a level with the eyes of the foremost horseman as he clambered up the slope. There was a great leap, a wild shout and Bill sprang forward, caught the horseman by waist and neck, and hung fast. Both men fell, and, locked together, went rolling down the slope, bringing up sharply against a tree trunk. There was much growling and struggling, much wild work and very little chivalry, and then, somehow, Bill Downer had his opponent's hands locked and was listening to wild cursing. For a moment he thought the noise came from his prisoner until, through a rift in the bushes, he saw the remaining Argentine coming, knife in hand, and that called to his mind a dim wondering and feeble speculation as to what had become of the knife he had seen in the hand of the man he held. At the same moment he became conscious of a slashing wound on his own shoulder from which the blood streamed plentifully, and with that, a sense of sleepiness. It took tremendous effort to wrench himself into a position in which he was half-crouching, half-kneeling on his enemy's chest and a persistent inner voice kept telling him that he had no plans, no plans whatever. He seemed to be desperately annoyed, too, because he was so tired and sleepy. Mysteriously, it seemed, another actor appeared, and it took a long time for Downer to realize that it was the Liverpool lad, spurred to encounter strange dangers by some mysterious notion of chivalry. The voice of the fellow recalled Bill Downer to life.

"Garn!" Bill heard him say, and saw him throw off his coat and roll up his sleeves, city slum fashion. Then there was expostulation and indignation expressed in throaty tones. "Fighting dago fashion, eh? Ought to be bloody well ashamed of yourselves, you ought. Two to one an' 'im down. Come up the 'ill an' fight fair, will yeahr?"

Meanwhile, Liverpool was flourishing his arms and making threatening gestures, but not moving. When a kind of abbreviated lightning flash shot athwart Downer's vision he did not realize its import until he heard Liverpool saying, "Yah! Chuckin' knives, eh?" Then the city lad resorted to primitive tactics. Not for nothing had he been a Hooligan gangster. A sudden energy possessed him and he fell to throwing stones at the Argentine with vicious force, accompanying each cast with a grunt and a "Take that, then! Uhh!"

Suddenly and swiftly the end came. Against the volley of stones the Argentine could not advance. For a moment he stood irresolute, then, with a curious movement, flung his hands apart.

"Bastante? Eh? Had bastante?" said Liverpool. "D'yer give in, eh?"

But there was no need for parley, and it was evident that no one had stomach for further fighting. Unhindered, Bill and his new ally clambered up the bank, released the trussed officer, mounted their horses and rode off, leading the pack horse with its treasure.

—5—

Eventually men became excited to admiration and imitation of the famous Bill, and the Governor of Punta Arenas offered a substantial reward for the arrest of "el Americano, Downer, salteador de caminos," and every Chilean, every Argentine, was on the watch. It was a hawk-faced fellow, an officer named Lopez, who had the fortune to capture Bill, and it was by the merest chance that he landed with seven men from a whale boat, a little to the north of Cape Nombre in the early morning of June 6th, 1895. The party was attached to the Sebastian Bay outfit, though their excursion was in the nature of a pleasure trip, the day, according to the notion of Señor Lopez, being unusually promising for the time of the year.

They came upon Bill Downer in a well-grassed vega, a great triangular piece of land wedged between sea and high baranca, and it came out afterwards that Bill was there in order that his horse, which was slightly lame, might rest and mend. Certainly, it was a thousand chances to one that any one would happen upon that particular place in all Tierra del Fuego, but the unlikely happened.

When the boat landed, Bill was barefoot, searching for shell fish and edible seaweed. A ridge of rock hid him from the party and he knew nothing of the presence of men there, until he heard the pistol crack for the hawk-faced officer with either great sapience and presence of mind, or else a natural lust for killing, shot the horse as soon as he set eyes on it. Hearing the shot, Bill went running, and, seeing the officer with his revolver and the men clustered a little in the rear, at once knew himself to be in desperate case. So he made for the baranca, seeking escape by climbing, but bullets began to pepper about him. Being a wise man, he stood stock still and threw up his hands. A one-sided parley followed, Bill being ignorant of Spanish, and at the end, the hawk-faced officer removed his glasses and wiped them carefully, then made a long speech in his hard, emphatic voice, from which Bill gathered that he was called upon to surrender.

Bill Downer stared at him steadily for a while, then said: "What else is there in thunder to do? It's eight to one, and me, I ain't got gun or nothin'."

So the officer gave a signal and three of the men approached Bill. Seeing that, Downer said, indignantly, "But all the same, you needn't think I'm going to be man-handled," and started to walk in the direction of the boat, calling as he went, to the officer to send a man up the beach for his shoes and things. To the request the officer paid no heed. Having reached the boat, Bill cocked a weather eye over the sky, then, with deliberation, took out his pipe and filled it. There was some mixed talking among the capturing party.

"Look'ee," said Bill, nodding darkly, "if you fellers want to get to Sebastian Bay with dry skins, you'd better walk, if I know mutton from goat."

He pointed, as he spoke, to a sulphurous-looking cloud in the southeast, and, by way of making his meaning clear, traced a jagged line in the air with his knotted, stubby forefinger. "See here. Bad weather's brewing, boys," he added, frowning and shaking his head.

But to them, landsmen, all weather signs meant nothing and the lurid sky with dark ragged clouds told no tale. True, they saw that the wind was rising, but, after all, the shelter of Sebastian Bay was but a few miles on the other side of the rocky point that jutted far out to the south. Hearing Bill's objection, Lopez regarded Downer for a moment with mild distaste, then turned to his men, bent on overriding the bad man's obstacles. One man, blustering a little, ventured to handle his revolver, and Bill stared at him fixedly with unamiable eye, whereat the fellow affected absent-mindedness. Still, it became clear to the highwayman that there was a concerted insistence everywhere which he could not easily defeat, and time was obviously too short for major controversies.

"Don't you go handling that silly thing, hombre," warned Bill, shaking his head in the direction of the man with a revolver; then fearing that his objections might have an appearance of fear, he said no more, but set his shoulder against the bow of the boat, prepared to aid the men in shoving off. Then everybody was busy at once, pushing and splashing and talking, eager to be gone. A weak ray of sunlight piercing the flying clouds considerably nerved the officer, who said something about the weather clearing up, and disposed himself in the stern seat, gathering his cloak comfortably about him. With a word of lofty command he motioned Bill to sit in the bows, and the helmsman by his side handed him a carbine.

Getting the boat out and under way was a difficult business, for the rowers were indifferent seamen and the freshening wind made a choppy sea. Scorn was writ large on Bill's countenance.

"I tell 'ee, 'twould be better to land and lay low a while," suggested Downer authoritatively, and almost as if he had something to do with the command. Then he added, by way of credentials, "I'm from Nova Scotia and know something about weather," and waved a hand to the southeast. Finding no response and thinking that the sullen clamor of the waves had drowned his words, and earnestly trying to make his captors understand, he summoned all his Spanish in an effort to explain that heavy weather was imminent. "Mucho viento pretty dam soon," he roared, and there was a note of exasperation in his voice.

To that the officer paid small attention, disregarding his prisoner with something of studied insolence, and gave a word of quite needless command. Then backs were bent to the oars, for it required heavy pulling because of the thumping seas, and Cape Nombre seemed to elongate itself, a milky churning disturbance marking the end of the reef. The most sea-ignorant in the boat knew that wide berth had to be given to that welter of water. But pull as they would what with wind and wave and tide, it seemed to Lopez that they were making no headway. Rather, they seemed to be drifting towards the white danger at the point of the cape. His eye fell on Bill and he called to him, bidding him take an oar, but to do that the prisoner stoutly refused.

"No, hombre, no! Plenty cuidado for viento," he yelled back in his lame Spanish, and turned his face windward again. Not for long would he look away from that fast moving bank of cloud. Lopez said no more then, well knowing the uselessness of a struggle to enforce his command, and he gripped hard the gunwale, and the boat, feeling the sweep of the wind outside the shelter of the point, ploughed into the rising sea.

With a roar the wind came, and rain, too, and sleet and snow, so that in a few minutes hands were numbed and faces stung. What was worse, ineptitude was at the helm and the boat broached to and shipped a light sea. A seaman would have laughed at it, but the men, half-scared, faltered and slackened in their rowing. So up in the bow rose Bill Downer. His tatooed chest was bare and his yellow hair streamed in the wind and lashed his face.

"Pull! Pull!" he roared, and, with open hand, struck the man nearest him a thundering blow on the shoulder, calling him a lazy hound. At once, the man was galvanized into great activity. But Bill did not sit again. From end to end of the rocking, leaping boat he went, stepping from thwart to thwart, striking this man, threatening that, and, snatching the oar from the steersman, with terrific strokes brought the boat round to head into the wind, roaring and cursing the while, an eye kept upon the lurid rack of sulphur-edged clouds. But the men were more fearful of the sullen roar, as of frenzied giants, that filled the air.

Half rising, one hand clutching tightly the gunwale, the other the seat, the officer said something, but what, in that rage of wind and water, none knew. As the boat leaped to meet a white-crested, green-gray monster of a roller, the officer spoke again, clutching at Bill's belt. With a swift hammer blow Downer struck him down and he fell into the bottom of the boat, the blood running from his face. For the briefest of moments there was doubt and vagueness in the rowers who saw the act, but no sign of slackening.

"Pull, you lazy hounds!" roared the prisoner. "Pull like hell," and they understood and obeyed, fearing him more than the danger that threatened. Straight into the gale he kept the boat, ever urging the men with huge shouts; straight into the tumbling sea and gray flying mist; straight into the shrieking babel. At a moment when there was a strange lull in which the fury of the storm seemed to have leaped over them, Bill Downer gave the steering oar to the helmsman, bidding him keep the course. Seeing that, the officer again spoke, again tugged at Bill's clothes, but the prisoner silenced him with a back-handed slap in the face.

"Leave this to me," he yelled in a rage of determination. "If not, overboard you go. Sabe?" And the officer said no more, crouching in the bottom of the boat, utterly cowed by this madman savior.

In another moment things were changed. Shouting, roaring, striking, Bill urged the men at the oars, sometimes laying hold himself and giving tremendous pulls. Then he was in the middle of the boat, and, with a convulsion of effort, dragged the little mast that was stowed away, absurdly enough, beneath the thwarts; stepped it, too, mastering cleverly the flying, snapping cordage and making all sound and taut. Soon up went the little jib and up went the reefed leg o' mutton sail, and, with a jerk like a whipped horse, the craft sprang into life, laying over with ear-splitting snappings, and crackings, tearing through the mad whirlpool of waters with a new purpose. So, with feet well braced, Bill stood at the stern again and took the steering oar, and the men, at his command, took in their oars. The gale gripped the boat then and the white, churning danger at the cape's end slid aft and lost itself in the thickening mist that veiled the land. Seaward they flew, into the storm and driving sleet with incredible swiftness; into a cold that soon glazed ropes with an ice skin and benumbed to the marrow the men no longer warmed with rowing.

High up, out of the murk and gloom, loomed the

head of Cape Sebastian, dark and stern and snow-patched, and dashing spray leaped up the face of the cliff like wraiths that strove to catch sight of human beings rushing to destruction. At the sight hearts sank, for they knew that the opening to the bay was long since passed, and awe-stricken and despairing the men crouched in the bottom of the boat, urged to action only when some crested wave broke, half-filling the craft with icy water. Then there was frantic baling. Once they shipped a crushing weight of water that carried away some of the oars and everything loose, and at that Bill laughed savagely.

All that short winter's day the storm was unabated, though there were fitful lulls as if some malignant *spottgeist* rested to gather force for the wreaking of more spite, and towards evening sharp and jagged mountains suddenly appeared, to merge a moment later in a gray cloud. The dark came with a rush and in the bosom of every man there was a black fear of death in a night world of wild tossing and shrieking, and the petition of those who called on their God was that strength might be with the wind-lashed man at the helm.

So came the long, black hours when everything vanished and the men knew nothing but the thunder of furious waters. Life was a monotony of blackness that blinded; of booming crested waves that leaped savagely out of the wall of darkness; of rapid, inky seas and sheeted spray; of dizzy climbings to wind-tossed pinnacles, to fierce slueings down interminable hissing slopes. Then came the shivering terror of a blue-white, long-shuddering lightning flash which ended in a thunderclap, a rolling, shattering explosion that shook the world. It was an explosion that released the hail demon, and, for hours, bullets of ice stung the tortured men to madness, made of the boat a thing of sheeted ice, turned ropes to rigid wire. Soon after, it was no longer utter darkness, but instead, a ghostly gray, and out of the roar of waters came a new sound, the howl of wave-beaten rock. Gray dawning showed them a mighty cliff, a vast and terrific thing like some dim-sighted leviathan, gaunt and threatening, that peered through the mist. And about the feet of the grim guardian of the straits of Le Maire was the mad turmoil of tide-torn, wind-whipped water.

So close were they that the black rocks were as vindictive heads thrust from the mad whirlpool to gloat over man's misery. Maliciously the heads shot from green-white waters to gaze and hide again; nearer they came until the brown, snaky hair that was tangling seaweed could be seen.

Bill Downer at the steering oar was like a giant, straining, wrestling, tugging to make the wind his ally against malevolent things of the sea. And he won, for the boat, in its changed direction, flew through the waters with prodigious speed so that the white foam curved above the bow to the height of a man's forearm.

Bravely though the little ship had done her task, it

was clear to Downer that she could not live in the crushing mass of waters ahead, the place where three oceans met and great winds battled, the place where wild seas boiled and seethed about Cape Horn. Yet there was one hope, a hope to dare greatly in an effort to reach Valentine Bay and, perchance, drop into the quieter waters in the lee of Tres Hermanos. An hour, then, of fierce battling in an effort to win across the shoal in a maelstrom of breaking crests, and suddenly scrub bushes leaped from gray backgrounds, and screaming gulls greeted them. But there came a racing, roaring sea astern, climbing steadily higher and higher, a giant billow to which all other giants were as dwarfs, a monster all white-crested that lifted the boat and bent over it embracingly—carried it forward—buried it.

So there was left but a sluggish thing, water-laden, and dead for the next green giant to laugh at, and the good fight was lost.

Nine men were in the boat and six found their way through the brown, slimy, tangling seaweed to a land of deep ravines and broken mountain; land of cold and desolation where gale follows gale and the heavens are hidden by swiftly-rolling great black clouds.

Those who escaped were cast ashore at the base of a long and narrow promontory, somewhat hook-shaped, where the water formed a kind of eddy, almost a whirlpool. The overturned boat was firmly wedged in the grip of a triple cleft rock, and, for a time, those on shore could see the officer and another man clinging to the keel. But not for long. Soon they were swept off, and, for a moment, could be seen struggling frantically; then they disappeared in a boiling tumult of white water. Not a man of the survivors but was bruised, scratched and torn, and one had a broken forearm. At first he was not conscious of his hurt, but soon he suffered exquisite pain.

It was a slashing gust of hail that drove the six from where they crouched in an angle of the cliff. Downer, naked save for his trousers, his hair water-matted and his beard gray with sand, took command. He had been sitting apart from the others, low in the kelp-strewn sand, gazing straight out to sea, and the beating ice roused him from his strange abstraction. He rose slowly and gave a deep sigh, "Thought I'd been on a drunk," he said. Then, summoning his Spanish in an effort to explain, he said with a grin, "Boraccho! Drunk!" He shook himself like a dog, in an effort to establish the world as a reality. One of the men said something, and crossed himself and made a motion to Bill. "That's all right," he said. "All right to say prayers, lads. But what's done can't be changed. Come on. Usuhaia now an' it's a long walk." With that he started off, went a few steps, then returned to support the man with the broken arm.

So began the walk along the desolate coast to the mission settlement of Beagle Channel and all that day they plodded on, sometimes floundering through bogs, at others threading their way across dismal valleys blocked with rotting tree trunks, and all the while, the wind, as night came on, cutting like swords of sharpness. Barren rock, ice, piercing wind and snow battled with each other, and the six tortured men struggled through the fray. A swooping albatross that swept over them, and floated up and away again against the wind, was the only thing that cheered them. Night was a black vastness of intensest cold. The storm of wind ceased and the Antarctic death was all about. In the air was the breath of icebergs, and life in the hearts of the men shrank to tiny sparks.

There was a time when some stood, refusing to go farther, and one threw himself down. But at that Downer became like a madman, raging, shouting, beating them with his fists. He drove them on as cattle are driven, with words, and blows, and cruel buffets. He urged them until he became voiceless and he struck at them until they cowered under his blows, and submitting, struggled onwards, though aching for death.

When dawn came, bringing its new cruel storm, the man with the broken arm gave up. It happened when they were crossing a valley strewn with great boulders set close together, most of them rounded, and all of them covered with an ice skin of glassy smoothness. Passing over a great rock, a black mass that stood like the monstrous back of some half-submerged mastodon, Gonzales slipped and fell, striking his broken arm on a sharp, jutting stone ridge. He gave a shrill scream, made a weak effort to rise, then surrendered. The four men, gaunt and hollow-eyed, watched him as he lay, too feeble, too disheartened, to offer aid. Bill Downer, who was a little way ahead, seeing the halt, returned.

"Up with you," he said hoarsely. Then, in his miserable Spanish, "Vamoose, hombre!"

But the fallen man made no effort other than to raise his head, gaze for a second at Downer, then let it fall again. Stooping, Bill lifted the man by the waist, but he hung limp, his head dangling, moaning piteously the while. Gently enough then, Bill replaced him on the rock and waved his hand for the others to go on their way.

"This here hombre's lost more livin' 'n he'll lose when he dies," he said to the rocks and sky. Then he turned to examine the man again, and rolled him over on his back. "Be a man!" he urged, and the exhausted fellow said something and made the sign of the cross. The four had stopped a few yards off and were watching listlessly. Bill regarded them searchingly, called on them to say something, but they were mute. Then slowly, he picked up a great, ice-crusted stone and held it above his head, poising it, but soon he let it fall. "Maybe 'twouldn't do," he mumbled. "It's but little luck I've had in my life, and maybe you're no luckier, and the black night's not far away. Still one smash and he'd rest easy. Then the thing is, there's to-morrow."

For a moment he stared stockishly, his mind refusing to work. Then there was a sudden change. As if the stricken man had been no weightier than a child, Downer picked him up and threw him over his shoulder, and, scrambling, stumbling, slipping, made his way over the treacherous stones to the other side of the valley. Down to the sea beach he went, the rest following, and laid his burden in the sand at the foot of a cliff.

"Off with your coats and things!" he commanded with a half-threatening gesture, fist clenched. The words meant nothing, but they understood. Soon every man stood as bare as he was, and Gonzales was wrapped and swathed in a bed of water-soaked garments. There was a gathering of seaweed, and a piling of it and half-putrified kelp about the wounded man. Mussels and fungi, too, Downer found, but the sick man feebly refused them.

Bill turned to the others. "Well," said he, "let's be getting under way and hurry. This here feller's got to be seen to and that soon." Then, looking down at the sick man, "Stick it out, lad, an' I'll come for ye. A man ought to prove himself by the punishment he can take, an' that's a fact. So long!"

Downer kept his word, as the men of Usuhaia know. For towards sunset of that day, as a *carretero* well wrapped in his poncho was urging his slow oxen home to the mission with a load of firewood on the lumbering cart, his horse trailing behind, he was astonished to see, on looking round, five men. At first he thought they were specters rounding the point, following him, for never had he seen men there, thus dragging their weary feet, naked and bleeding, over the stony beach. Four of them were half-dead, and, strangely enough, wept at sight of him. But the fifth, he thought, was crazed by hardships endured. For while the four slowly crawled upon the heap of driftwood in the cart, the fifth, with threats, robbed him of his poncho, his coat, his shirt; took and devoured ravenously his bread; stole his horse. Then, still acting savagely, he mounted and disappeared in the direction from which he had come.

And that night, when doors in the settlement houses were fast shut because of the raging, cutting wind, when those who sat about the stoves wrapped were yet chilled, when men who knew the land spoke with dread of the morrow because of the wild morning weather, there was a great barking of dogs and the noise of a horse and of a shouting man.

I saw it all, for I was at Usuhaia that night. I saw Bill Downer, barefooted and naked to the waist, a blue-eyed Viking, all blood-stained and bruised and thorn-torn. He was leading the horse he had taken from the *carretero* and in the saddle was the wounded and tortured Gonzales, warmly wrapped, but haggard as one who had seen the Antarctic death. And when we rushed out into the dark in the knee-deep snow from the bright and clean mission room, all eager to do things, Bill Downer seemed irritated, and, turning to me, reproached me, saying that I should know better than to make a fuss.

"All I want," he said, "is a good night's sleep and

something hot to drink. And I got to get a horse somehow in the morning. Things has been too hot lately."

—6—

Next morning Bill was gone and two of the best horses had disappeared. There was some talk of following him, for a time, but when it became known that a revolver and ammunition were missing, men's eyes met and no more was said. It suddenly became clear that a land of confused hills and rocky valleys, of thick bushes and tangled low trees, was no place for man hunting. One man alone surveyed the map, murmuring the names of places as he traced a course, then, with a gesture of impatience turned away and surveyed the roaring stove.

"Poor devil, let him go," he said.

"To begin with, there's nothing else that we can do," grumbled another.

So Bill went somewhere, somehow met his dilapidated young man from Liverpool whose name was Ned Williams, and soon things came to a focus so that men and gold were together. But to an outsider, it seems all foggy and monstrous how things fell out; how they evaded pursuit, for there was at least one case of pursuit when they stole a horse from Gente Grande after some wrangle and scuffle with a couple of shepherds; how they survived the sudden blizzard. At any rate they reached Porvenir Bay and there took ship. Nor was

In the saddle was the wounded and tortured Gonzales

there further news of them until the men of *El Corcino* took their tale to Punta Arenas.

—7—

At Porvenir Bay one night, the *Chilota,* a one-master, lay at anchor. Captain Olsen and Andrew Andersen were ashore at the Greek's place and the other member of the crew, Joe Taaffe, was enjoying his sense of proprietorship. He had, as captain *pro tem,* given himself, as crew, freedom of the captain's cabin after washing decks, and was stretched out on the carpeted floor with a pillow under his head, reading a paper-backed novel and smoking a stout pipe the while. To enjoy his comfort the more, there were times when he went on deck to take a look at the dark shadows of the hills, the black waters or the brilliant stars, and, having done that, there was a sense of elation that he could, at the very moment he chose, plunge into the cabin again. It was a pleasure to throw himself down to dream, and always, his dream was the same. Some day, he, Joe Taaffe, would own a one-masted schooner-rigged boat similarly appointed. It would be painted like old man Olsen's *Chilota.* The cabin would be much the same. Certainly there would be an octagonal-shaped clock and a similar folding table; a shelf of books, too; a brass-railed bunk; a mirror set in a closet door; an enameled washing outfit. For that cabin represented the sum total of his earthly ambition; the little ship dominated his dreams. Going about his work as deck hand, cargo trimmer, stevedore, cook, rigger, blacksmith, ship's carpenter, painter, steward, handy man, navigator, he often amused himself in trying to figure the entire cost of the outfit. Against it he set the sum of his monthly earnings, ten dollars and keep. Ten dollars into, say five thousand, goes five hundred, and five hundred divided by twelve gives forty-one and eight over. Coming down to hard facts, that meant forty-one years and eight months of life. So, Joe being twenty-four years of age, might, as he saw it, at the age of sixty-five and a little over, be able to offer old Olsen his price and bid him go about his business. The only trouble was that fact and theory failed to hang together. For two years he had been on the *Chilota* and there were no two hundred and forty dollars to his credit anywhere. There had been incidental expenditures—odd things bought, and sprees—especially sprees. Somehow, sprees accounted for too much. And Punta Arenas was full of places where jollity reigned. Mulach's, for instance, where one sat and looked out over the sea and saw, now and then, a steamer—and Jack Bean's, untidy but jolly —and Mattlitche's place. . . . So long as the pay he seemed able to command was what it was and schooners were the price that they were, every spree, it was clear, was a setback. Well, then, there would be no sprees. That is, there would be one good, last one on the next trip to Punta Arenas and thenceforth and forever after, strict sobriety. So Joe turned to his novel, pondered a while over the love troubles of Lord Halliwell, turned down the wick of the copper lamp to give his eyes a chance, listened a while to the soft lapping water, sighed in utter comfort and slept.

On Monroe Point, less than half a mile away, two men figured—men who knew that they would be close-pressed soon because of the leather bag of gold, for neither Bill Downer nor his new partner, Ned Williams of Liverpool, contemplated risk.

"We got to do the trick now," said Bill. "It's got to be done afore the tide starts runnin'."

"You're a game un," said Ned, and stood with his weak chin hanging loose. "'Strewth, I didn't think you meant it when you first said it," he added after a pause, but Bill took no notice of the remark. Neither praise nor blame ever touched him.

"Doubtless there's three aboard. There used to be," sounded Bill's quiet voice in the dark. "Two of us must manage 'em."

Ned Williams had a vague feeling that all might not be so easy as Bill seemed to take for granted, but he buried his doubts and objections. The adventure had something of the appearance of a disciplined attack and the Liverpool lad felt safe when obeying orders. He was of the mass, the mass born to be welded by a few of strange power. When doubt arose, an order given comforted him.

"You tell me what to do an' I'll do it," he said into the dark.

"Turn the horses loose," was Bill's order. "But see to it that you strip off the gear first. No need to let 'em suffer."

"A course, we cut off our chances that way if things go wrong," said Liverpool Ned.

A growl came from the darkness in reply—an ominous kind of growl, a growl that held in it the threat of something more dangerous. At the sound of it, Ned Williams had the same feeling of fear that always possessed him at the first rumblings of an approaching thunderstorm. He sprang to his feet and went to work on the horses, and the animals, being freed, nickered softly, ran a few yards and commenced to graze. The gear was neatly stacked above high-water mark.

"All done, boss," said Williams.

"Strip then," said Bill laconically.

"Golly!"

"Well, you can't swim in big boots and a leather coat, can you? And you're not goin' to carry 'em, are you?" Bill's words brought a sense of irrevocability to the Liverpool lad. Without any accent, without appearance of interest even, Downer added: "Guess you don't want to be drowned."

"Blime, no!" answered Ned. "But it struck me kinder funny, goin' into a fight without any clothes on, like."

Downer was unconcernedly undressing.

"Look here, Liverpool," he said. "There's lots of

games in this life what you don't tackle till you come to 'em. Don't try to plan out your life in neat order like them Dutch gardeners plan their flower beds. Man's got to be quick turnin' like a fox and not all cased up in his shell like a armadillo. See? Me, I'm going through with this. If you got any doubts, stay here takin' your chance. You can have your share of the gold in that case, and all the horses. But me, I'm going."

There was an air of finality about the speaker that puzzled Ned. He stood looking at his dim shadow for a little, taking in what Downer had said, then commenced to strip.

Barefooted, it was difficult, walking over the slippery and weed-covered stones, Ned carrying the gold and Bill shouldering a heavy piece of driftwood, but suddenly the adventure seemed to strike the Englishman as being funny and he commenced to talk. Bill curtly bade him hold his tongue.

The chill of the far southern water made them shiver. A plunge would not have been so bad. As it was, there was nothing for it but to wade deeper, inch by inch, until they were in water deep enough to float the driftwood, across which they placed the bag of gold. Then it was swimming and pushing the log, with much trouble with the stringy, slimy kelp that caught at them like snakes. Soon they forgot everything but the job in hand.

The white ship leaped into visibility suddenly and

then Ned found himself nervous with strained expectation. He was like a shell-shocked man in a thunderstorm. It seemed to him that the thing to be expected was a revolver shot from the deck, and his own gurgling struggle. When Bill touched his arm, he gave a low exclamation of dismay. The Nova Scotian, being a man of small imaginings, felt no such fears. He pushed the log to the bows and found the anchor chain, whispered to Ned to stay where he was, holding fast to both log and chain, and went up and disappeared inboard.

It did not surprise him to find the deck deserted, and he flitted light as a cat from stem to stern, staring with a sort of wonder when he saw the sleeper in the cabin, lamp at his head and book by his side. Next he leaned far out, over the rail, all alert to catch any sound of an approaching boat, but there was no stir except the faint whisper of the smooth water sweeping the hull. Being satisfied, he returned to the little scuttle through which he had seen the sleeper, and slid the cover, making all fast. At the bow he dropped a line, slid down the chain into the water and secured the bag of gold, which being done, he clambered back on deck, after touching his ally to follow, and together they hauled the treasure aboard.

"What about the crew?" whispered Liverpool.

"Have done with the whispering!" boomed Bill in his heavy bass and the sudden shattering of the silence made the other jump. "Tend to orders now." Then he beckoned to Ned with a jerk of the head, and indicated the cabin. "Go down," he said, "and call the other fellow."

Of course, Joe Taaffe was amazed at what he saw when awakened, and more amazed when, reaching the deck, he was addressed by what he immediately recognized as an authoritative voice.

"I'm sailing master, lad," said Bill.

To be sure, Joe looked at him with respect. Strange things happened in Magellan waters, but there was a large element of doubt in the present case. Had the self-styled sailing master appeared properly clothed, things would have had another aspect. So Joe searched his mind, to fall back, as he usually did, on the world of fiction. He had not read Charles Reade for nothing. So he coughed a little and said, not without a touch of the dramatic:

"Yes, sir. But, to be sure, what is your appointment to the command?"

"Bring up that there binnacle light and I'll show you," said Bill.

Joe obeyed and the Liverpool lad dragged to the light the treasure bag, as Bill had ordered.

"Heft it!" ordered Downer, and Joe Taaffe bent to raise the sack, tested the weight of it, found it altogether exceptional, and, having done all that, stood regarding Downer with an air of abstraction. "It's all gold," said the self-appointed captain. "San Sebastian gold. If you want to share in—"

He left the sentence unsaid and the three stood there in the light of the lamp, Joe Taaffe in his shirt sleeves and corduroys and white alpagatas, Ned Williams jerkily active but unclothed, Downer leaning against the mast, his arms akimbo, also unclothed.

After a little while Downer said, gravely:

"I'm sailing master on this here craft. If you want to play the game square and join in, you'll get a third when we get there, and if—"

"Get where?" asked Joe.

"Africa. South Africa," answered Downer. "Cape Town and then Kimberly for me."

"Gee whiz!" exclaimed Ned Williams.

"And the alternative?" asked Joe.

"What d'yer mean?" asked Downer in return. "What's alternative?"

"I mean what if I don't want to join in?" said Joe.

"Why, you go ashore right now and that ends it," declared Downer.

"I'd like to be in it," conceded Joe, "but the truth is that I'd rather work on wages."

"What d'yer get now?" asked the sailing master.

"Ten and found," Joe said, quietly enough.

"On wages you get fifty and found, so get busy and decide," came from Downer, a trifle impatiently.

"Righto," said Joe cheerfully. "I'm with you."

"Hunt up clothes for us, then. Bring me a pipe and tobacco and matches. Then get things clear for sailing and we'll drop out on the tide. Suppose your lines is all in runnin' order?"

The new crew was steadily efficient, good sailors all, and at the turn of the tide, they made the S-shaped channel and found the Straits handsomely, under a light breeze. The next evening they dropped anchor abreast of Elizabeth Island, where they went ashore to fill the water casks.

Now, the only good spring on that island is at the northeastern end where the land ends in a high wedge-shaped point, on both sides of which is excellent anchorage. It was there that Magellan dropped anchor for the first time in the Straits. But because of the high ridge, it is quite possible for two ships to be within a quarter of a mile of each other, yet for neither to know of the other's presence, and so it was that the men of the *Chilota* knew nothing of the anchoring of the little gunboat, *El Corcino*. For Downer had sailed the *Chilota* between Cape Negro and the butt of Elizabeth Island, while *El Corcino* had approached from the east and taken a course heading outside the island, bound for Punta Arenas.

The trio on the *Chilota* having finished their watering, sat on the little deck, enjoying the breeze and the sparkle of sunset sea, smoking the excellent Brazilian tobacco that had been the pride of old man Olsen, nor were the hearts of them any heavier than the hearts of the two men who had left the gunboat to stretch their legs on shore. As for the latter, what they imagined to be the intense loneliness of the Magellan country had somewhat depressed them, and it was with a distinct shock that, from the top of the ridge, they beheld the little white ship. "I think," said one of the two, pointing, "that is Captain Olsen's little ship, so there may be something amusing in a visit paid to him."

So the two officers went down the hill and reached the little cove in which was their boat and four men, blue and white clad, and soon the little craft was speeding merrily, the gay flag a-flutter.

Had it not been for that flag, things might have turned out differently, but seeing it, as the boat came in sight round the point, suspicion seized the hearts of Downer and his crew.

"Wherever you see that kind of thing, there's trouble ahead," said Joe.

"And never a gun on board to protect our rights," complained the Liverpool lad.

"Get busy," said Downer, and there was immediate activity with sail and anchor.

But the distance that the boat had to travel was short and the men rowers were young and powerful, nor, in that bay, was there much sea room. So it came about that by a combination of luck and ability, the *Corcino's* boat came alongside, the rowers laid hold of the rail of the little ship and the *Chilota* swung to the breeze and in full sight of the *Corcino* with a vigorous parasite hanging close to her side. Seeing the strange manner in which their friendly overtures had been received, the officers were full of suspicion, which suspicion became a verity when one of the men recognized Downer and called out:

"El salteador Be-el. Him I saw at San Sebastian."

Out came two revolvers then, and the two Argentine naval officials saw visions of preferment for the capture of the outlaw. As though they were unaware of the trouble, Ned and Joe did their work, and the little ship gathered way, slipping neatly across the calm water. So they came in sight of the *Corcino* and the younger officer fired his revolver in the air. As though it were an echo, there came a responding shot from the gunboat; then another, and another.

Then it was that Bill Downer stepped back a couple of paces. The men in the little boat saw his head disappear as he dipped, and the thought flashed across both their minds that the renowned salteador was not the fearless fighter that he had been depicted.

"Surrender yourself!" called out one of the officers.

Bill might have heard and he might not. It was impossible to tell, for he made no sign. The freshening breeze had caught the sails and Joe was at the tiller. Bill Downer took in all at a sweeping glance, the gunboat, the course, the position of Martha Island, which was little more than a great rock, and then he stooped and took hold of the anvil that was on deck. A wrench and a tug, strained muscles and swelling veins, and he had it loose and high lifted above his head. So at the rail he stood, and the men in the little boat saw and cowered, scurrying to bow and to stern, save one who held on pluckily. For a moment the weight of iron was poised, then, with a shout of wild exultation, Bill let go and the mass crashed through the bottom of the boat. Grinning, Bill laid hold of a stay and waved a hand in farewell to the men swimming about their foundered craft, and before the shot came from the gunboat that the men of the *Chilota* expected, the little white ship had put Martha Island between herself and danger.

•   •   •   •   •   •   •

Of the voyage across the Atlantic by way of the Falkland Islands there is little to tell. They touched at Port Stanley and took in provisions, and in due time they made Cape Town. It was there that I met them and heard what I have set down. I said Cape Town, but should have said between there and Johannesberg, for we were on our way together to join Dr. Jamieson in his raid. At Vlakfontein, Bill got a Boer bullet in his chest, one of twenty-one who died that first day of the year 1896.

THE END

HV
6665
G7F7
1970

Date Due